On the eve of the atonement

On the eve

of the

atonement

Peter Trumper

 EVANGELICAL PRESS

EVANGELICAL PRESS
12 Wooler Street, Darlington, Co. Durham, DL1 1RQ, England

© Evangelical Press 1994
First published 1994

British Library Cataloguing in Publication Data available

ISBN 0 85234 321 3

Scripture quotations in this publication are from the Authorized (King James) Version.

Printed and bound in Great Britain at the Bath Press, Avon.

Contents

Foreword

I am pleased to have been invited to contribute a foreword to *On the eve of the atonement*. We are living in an age when countless books are being published; I venture to suggest that this one is different and therefore should find a place on the bookshelves of all who would understand just what happened prior to Calvary. In these pages Dr Peter Trumper vividly sets forth God's ordained events, the rebellion of wicked men and the agonies of the man Christ Jesus.

All who are acquainted with the author will remember him for his forthright faithful expositions of Scripture, and for his fearless defence of the historic faith. This valuable volume has been written by one of the most spiritually profound minds I have come across, yet a man who is in much physical weakness.

It is a great mystery why this beloved brother should be stricken down with multiple sclerosis in a day when such preaching is needed. However, in the providence of God this has given Dr Trumper the opportunity to write, now he is not able to exercise his gifts in public ministry.

I fully recommend this splendid book, which will enlighten the mind, spark off sermons for the preacher and remind every reader of the incalculable cost of our redemption.

Bearing shame and scoffing rude,
In my place condemned he stood;
Sealed my pardon with his blood:
    Hallelujah! What a Saviour!

Peter Hulland
Pastor, Stanton Lees Chapel,
Derby

Prologue

Deep within eternal ages past, 'while as yet he had not made the earth, nor the fields, nor the highest part of the dust of the world' (Prov. 8:26), the Being of the triune God conceived a plan. At the appointed time, he would establish a nation in the midst of a fallen world, whose beauty would be holiness (1 Peter 2:9). It would be mighty and glorious, sharing in the eternal and gracious love experienced within the Godhead (John 17:24), transcending even the angelic hosts whose myriads everlastingly encircle his throne, adoring and worshipping him (Isa. 6:1-3). Its innumerable citizens (Rev. 7:9-10), each one a beloved and precious jewel in his crown (Mal. 3:16-17), were already known to him, the heavenly ledger filled with their names written large (Rev. 20:15).

With the cry, 'I delight to do thy will, O my God' (Ps. 40:8), the Son ventured forth from glory as a token of his love for the Father, the Originator of the plan, and affection for those whose names he had read in the great book of life (John 10:14-15). Passing through the angelic ranks, and clothing himself in flesh (Heb. 2:9-18), he entered the world, having been conceived by the Spirit in a virgin's womb (Gal. 4:4-5). His name, which heaven supplied, was Jesus (Matt. 1:21-25); his task, the pivot around which the Father's plan revolved (John 7:29).

From an early age he had been in possession of a Messianic consciousness, the awareness that he must be engaged in his 'Father's business' (Luke 2:49), the most important part of which would be his sacrificial atoning death to secure the redemption of those names

(John 10:11,15), part of fallen mankind requiring rescue (1 Cor. 15:22). Now the moment, the 'hour' (John 12:27), he had anticipated throughout his adult life had arrived. He had dreaded it, wrestled in prayer over it (Matt. 26:42) and wept about it (Heb. 5:7).

The view from Olivet

A few days before his crucifixion, Jesus sought a moment of quiet seclusion from the agitated crowds and the cacophonous excitement surrounding the temple precincts. As if carried along on the swelling of an incoming high tide, he had ridden into Jerusalem that Sunday surrounded by a sea of ecstatic faces, gesticulating arms and waving palms. It was no occasion for those who wished to remain silent, for rippling through the mass of humanity which filled the streets and alleyways to overflowing was a paean of praise: 'Blessed be the King that cometh in the name of the Lord: peace in heaven, and glory in the highest' (Luke 19:38). Then followed the expected disagreeable response from the ever-present priests (Luke 19:39). By contrast, the quietness on Mount Olivet was refreshing.

From that vantage-point, Jesus was able to see the network of Jerusalem's narrow streets like ruts in a field, and the small houses huddled together as if for support. To his right stood the Castle of Antonia, strong and austere like the empire itself, but Jesus' gaze was not directed towards it. He was more interested in the temple, an even grander edifice which displayed its magnificence for all to see. It rose high in the centre of the foreground landscape, dwarfing all around, his Father's house of prayer and yet a den for thieves! With a display of holy anger he had cleared it out three years before (John 2:14-16), and would do so again (Luke 19:45).

But buildings, even the temple, were not Jesus' main preoccupation that day, for he was always more concerned with people. Jerusalem lay before him, a hive of activity, and from where he sat could be seen her citizens moving restlessly in every direction engaged in their daily business, like the proverbial grasshoppers over which almighty God rules with sovereign power (Isa. 40:22).

The cloudless sky stretched out above their heads as far as the eye could see like a massive blue dome, flowers bedecked every hill and the land was a splash of colour, but the people's thoughts were not of the Creator, since they feared the power of Rome more than the awesomeness of God (Matt. 6:26-29). They admired Herod's architectural temple masterpiece in honour of Cæsar (Matt. 24:1), but paid scant heed to the purity of divine worship within it (Matt. 21:13). They had even forgotten their heritage, the *raison d'être* for Israel's existence, and when shortly afterwards their leaders were reminded of it by a choice servant of God they killed him (Acts 7). It was all far removed from the ideal, from what Jesus valued, appreciated, reflected and loved. The persistent realization of this fact saddened him deeply.

As he sat on the slopes of Olivet contemplating the scene, his thoughts were directed towards heaven. Soon he would be returning to the Father, having accomplished the divine mission originated within the heavenly council (John 17:4-5). From the mount he had a view of the distant Golgotha, the venue ordained for the climax of the Father's plan and purpose. Within a few days he would be confronting the horrors of the bloodstained cross and all that implied in terms of paying the price of sin — but after that what joys awaited him! (Heb. 12:2). The disciples were to hear him pray along those lines: 'Father, I will that they also, whom thou hast given me, be with me where I am; that they may behold my glory, which thou hast given me: for thou lovedst me before the foundation of the world' (John 17:24).

The wonders of God's love

Throughout the few years of his time among men no one had been, or could have been, capable of understanding what it meant for Jesus to have intimately experienced the unreserved, unceasing and eternal love of God the Father. The sinners across the way from where he sat were so taken up with temporal values that, if questioned, they would have been astonished to learn that he considered they knew little about love, and nothing about eternal love. Sin has blurred the essential beauty, the exquisite joyfulness, of an experience which has its roots in God (Gen. 1:26). What they thought of as love at times reached depths of satisfaction, even heights of ecstasy, but like a flower valued for its colour, shape and perfume, it was soon to die, as those taking pleasure from it recognized. What did those sinners know about the love of God? What had they really tasted of love itself? Sin had marred them, locked and barred them out from what they might have known, and now in most cases would never know. The thought brought tears to Jesus' eyes.

Divine love filled every recess deep within the mysteries of eternal ages past, the unhindered outpouring of pure affection between the three Persons within the Godhead. God is the ultimate and only love (1 John 4:8). It was he who brought the angelic hosts into being, that the truest and purest love of all could be shared in the sublime act of worship (Rev. 4:10-11). Only those who have experienced love can express their devotion in worshipping the God of love, and its abyss is bottomless. Before time, when man had no part to play, the essence of eternal awareness was the sublimity of rapturous devotion. Father, Son and Holy Spirit shared the perfection of their love in the oneness of their being and expressed this divine quality to the created hosts, who in turn responded with adoration (Isa. 6:1-3).

It was love which drew up the blueprint for the design of the most elaborate masterpiece of all, the entire universe. The divine Wisdom, the Son, the precise expression of the mind of the Father and the effulgence of his glory (Heb. 1:1-3), was present when the beauty, unity and being of the cosmos were first realized (Prov. 8:23-32). With the deft touch of divine fingers the brilliant sun and fascinating moon were ordained to hang in the vast blackness of space (Ps. 8:3-4) whilst myriads of twinkling galaxies, each single star carefully designed and named (Ps. 147:4), were to be arranged in their orbit with mathematical precision and by detailed laws. The result was not a Big Bang, but a noise much louder than that. God spake, and the Word obedient to the mind behind the command brought all things into being within the framework of six full days (Exod. 20:11).

That same love of God placed man upon the earth, the pivot of his creative act out of earth's dust (Gen. 2:7), so precious in the divine estimation that he was made in the image and likeness of the Creator (Gen. 1:26). It was the injury to the love relationship inflicted by the fall of man that produced in God the sharp reaction one would expect, demanding vindication of his perfect righteousness. Man was driven from his presence and fellowship was broken (Gen. 3:24)

Equally, God's profound love for his chief creation desired and planned man's redemption, complete reconciliation with the one offended and restoration of the love-filled, love-orientated, unity between God and man experienced in Eden. It is a love 'vast, unmeasured, boundless, free', for it included the sending of no less a person than his own Son to make the supreme sacrifice (John 3:16) in bearing the curse of the broken law in his own body. He fulfilled its just demands in the full glare of the Father's watchful eye (Gal. 3:10,13). Paradise had been lost, but it was also to be regained.

The majesty of Christ

If only the sons as well as the daughters of Jerusalem could have understood the language of nature in those final few days prior to Jesus' crucifixion, they would have quickly learned to value the figure sitting alone on the hillside. When God asked Job, 'Where wast thou when I laid the foundations of the earth?' (Job 38:4), the noble patriarch was made to appreciate the paucity of his understanding of matters eternal and divine. He knew God more intimately than most, but when God asked him over seventy questions about the realm of nature he found he was grossly ignorant (Job 38-41). Christ could have answered them all with ease, for 'By him were all things created, that are in heaven, and that are in earth, visible and invisible, whether they be thrones, or dominions, or principalities, or powers: all things were created by him, and for him' (Col. 1:16).

The one sitting on the hillside was the one at whose command, when his majestic presence gives vent to his displeasure, thunders roll and lightning flashes, powerful winds cut a swathe through landscapes and devastation lies everywhere. When he roars the earth quakes and cracks and diminutive men and their possessions are swallowed whole, but when he whispers the cattle graze peace-fully upon a thousand hills (Ps. 50:10-11) and the fallow deer roam safely (Ps. 29). After all, 'He is before all things, and by him all things consist' (Col. 1:17).

Jesus weeps over Jerusalem

These thoughts must have circulated in Jesus' mind as he stared across at Jerusalem before him, a city over which more tears have been shed than any other in history, and yet also one capable of engendering more joy than any other. From the day David captured it from the Jebusites, establishing it as his city (2 Sam. 5:7), men had yearned and fought over it. When the exiled Jews in Babylon were asked to sing their native songs they refused, their homesickness being acute: 'If I forget thee, O Jerusalem, let my right hand forget her cunning. If I do not remember thee, let my tongue cleave to the roof of my mouth; if I prefer not Jerusalem above my chief joy' (Ps. 137:5-6). The city was the central place of worship. There stood Mount Moriah, where Abraham had been commanded by God to offer his son Isaac as a sacrifice (Gen.22:2) and David had received a visitation from the angel of the Lord (2 Sam. 24). Upon that spot Solomon had built the temple (2 Chron. 3:1) in which the most holy place housed the ark, the symbol of God's covenant with Israel (1 Kings 8:6-11).

One cannot imagine Jesus' feelings as he pondered the situation from the heights of Olivet, but the private agony experienced is etched upon his solemn words: 'If thou hadst known, even thou, at least in this thy day, the things which belong unto thy peace! But now they are hid from thine eyes' (Luke 19:42). Israel's day was at its twenty-third hour, the time of the 'visitation' was almost over (Luke 19:44). God had visited the nation in the person of his Son, but soon it would crucify him. When the love of God is rejected, what remains? Jesus wept over Jerusalem as the minutes ticked on and divine retribution drew closer.

The day of the 'dry tree' (Luke 23:31) was one generation away, but the Son of God was alone in anticipating it (see 'Epilogue'). Jerusalem, like certain cities of modern times, was no stranger to tragic events, her history being full of them. The Assyrian armies had swarmed over the hills of Samaria towards her like wolves upon the fold in the eighth century before Christ; the Chaldeans had swept through her in the sixth; the Syrians and Romans followed suit years later. Jerusalem's citizens were almost hardened to the prospect of any further turmoil, although it did not ease the pain of enduring it when it arrived.

In the meantime, within her walls daily conversations continued of a more mundane nature: the Roman occupation, social deprivation and general dissatisfaction with the status quo. However, Jesus' grief was not limited to the fact of his rejection by the people he loved and who for him were 'as sheep having no shepherd' (Matt. 9:36), although that was by far the chief reason. His love also dictated his concern for the catastrophe which lay ahead. Jesus knew what they were to expect, and from whom they were to expect it: 'For the days shall come upon thee, that thine enemies shall cast a trench about thee, and compass thee round, and keep thee in on every side' (Luke 19:43).

By this time the disciples had joined Jesus on the mount. They were intrigued by his recent reaction to their typical Jewish appreciation of the temple grandeur. Instead he had alarmed them by calmly warning of its impending destruction; in fact he insisted that, so extensive would be the demolition of the temple, it would be razed to the ground (Matt. 24:2). Needless to say, the disciples desired an explanation to satisfy their curiosity, and Jesus supplied it (Matt. 24). These men, as would be expected, were the first to hear his warning. Jerusalem had less than forty years to heed it.

1.
Beside ruffled waters

Hatred and suspicion stalked the streets and dusty alleyways of Jerusalem that Thursday evening. The proud city had experienced numerous moments of tension during her long history, but nothing quite like this. An unwelcome atmosphere hung like a thick mist over everything, resulting in the kind of eerie silence soldiers must experience prior to a battle. Nothing untoward appeared to be happening, yet everyone within Jerusalem understood that appearances were not to be believed, for the darkness harboured treachery of a peculiar kind.

Earlier that day Jesus had given instructions to his apostles, Peter and John, to prepare the passover feast (Luke 22:8). That meant the purchasing of the paschal lamb, the unleavened bread and the bitter herbs. It also implied the slaughtering of the lamb within the temple precincts according to the law (Exod. 12:5-10). Then the lamb would have been roasted and the herbs especially prepared.

The two friends enquired about the venue for the annual occasion and received an unusual reply. Once in the city they were to look for a man doing a woman's work, carrying a pitcher of water. He was expecting them and would guide them to the meeting-place, and once inside the house a signal would be given to the owner which he as a follower of Jesus would understand. The signal was: 'The Master saith, My time is at hand' (Matt. 26:18). Then, no doubt when recognition had been acknowledged, the actual message was given: 'The Master saith unto thee, Where is the guestchamber, where I shall eat the passover with my disciples?' (Luke 22:11). In the encounter, Jesus' name was not mentioned but merely hinted at for the benefit of friendly ears. It was that kind of situation, and something similar had occurred the previous Sunday (Matt. 21:1-3).

Once dusk had arrived, Jesus and the twelve intimate friends walked the two miles from Bethany, where they had been staying, and quietly slipped into the city (Matt. 26:6-20). They made their way through what were probably deserted streets, for the citizens were preparing for the following day's festivities, towards the place chosen as the setting for the Last Supper, a furnished upper room tucked away from prying eyes. Did it belong to Mark's mother? (Acts 12:12). Whether it did or not, little did anyone realize it would become the most famous upper room in history!

The room was large and easily accommodated thirteen men. The scene was a friendly one, in sharp contrast to the heavy atmosphere in the street outside, and there were all the signs of gracious hospitality: the jar full of water with the accompanying towel placed by the door to ease the travellers' weary feet (Luke 7:44), the table spread with generous provisions and the triclinia laid with cushions for the guests upon which they would recline. They did so in the customary manner, turned towards the table with their feet stretched out behind them. The sight created the impression that a comfortable and cosy evening spent with a close friend lay ahead for these privileged disciples. It was not to be. Instead, they were about to be confronted with naked truth about themselves which, for their own good, was to prove uncomfortable.

Disputes over precedence among the disciples

The first intimation they had of this was immediately they had taken their places around the table. This normally simple act, though, was not without its difficulties for the twelve, for reclining as near to Jesus as possible had become something of a status symbol! How often during the three years they had walked with him, had they argued among themselves which of them was considered by Jesus to be the most important, even the greatest! (Mark 9:33-37). Such was their wilful pride that they had not only whispered their discussions, but had shamelessly enquired of him about the matter (Matt.18:1-6).

So important was the topic to them that the brothers John and James went further. On one notable occasion, they drew Jesus aside and petitioned him like children: 'Master, we would that thou shouldest do for us whatsoever we shall desire.' Jesus must have smiled, but graciously heard their plea: 'Grant unto us that we may sit, one on thy right hand, and the other on thy left hand, in thy glory' (Mark 10:35,37). Of course, such a request could not be granted, but Jesus' refusal did not prevent them from trying again, this time through the intervention of their mother (Matt. 20:20-21). Even the dying thief was more humble. He just wanted to be remembered, believing himself too unworthy for heavenly distinction (Luke 23:42).

The questing after position always appeared to raise its head at the most inopportune moments, when Jesus was acutely aware of the close proximity of his crucifixion. Their selfishness and childish behaviour stood in sharp contrast to his awesome humility, his self-sacrificing spirit to their egocentricity. A well-known example of this was just prior to Jesus' final journey from the north to Jerusalem, when 'the time was come that he should be received up' (Luke 9:51). It was clear to everyone that the turning-point for him had arrived; a glance at his face should have told the story, with determination and dedication etched upon it. The climax of his ministry upon earth was approaching quickly, with all that meant in terms of infinite suffering and pain which was unique to him. But instead of seeking to understand or sympathize, however inadequately, those nearest and dearest to him were engaged in the usual controversy over which of them was the greatest. How patient Jesus was when rebuking them, not with harsh words as he might have done, but with the visual aid of a child placed before them: 'He that is least among you all, the same shall be great' (Luke 9:48).

Now in the upper room, with Calvary a mere few hours away, the persistent squabbling failed to have a respite, a situation which obviously grieved Jesus, especially on such a night when he was contemplating his impending crucifixion as well as the reasons for it. In fact, such was the rivalry among his friends that Jesus probably felt obliged to point each one to the place he was to occupy at the table. Sadly, the brethren could not be trusted to graciously work it out among themselves. If their Master allotted the places for them this may have been the reason why the squabbling broke out between them later in the evening (Luke 22:24-27). Even after three years of walking with Jesus they had failed to grasp this basic aspect of his teaching, that 'Whosover therefore shall humble himself as this little child, the same is greatest in the kingdom of heaven' (Matt. 18:4).

Jesus washes the disciples' feet

Suddenly, as the twelve were reclining comfortably, Jesus arose from his position and walked silently and slowly to the large water-jar by the door upon which was the customary towel ready for use. To their amazement he began removing his clothing and continued doing so until he was dressed only in the towel, which acted as a loincloth. As they watched with astonishment, he poured water from the jar into a basin and quietly approached the nearest disciple, knelt in front of him and began washing his feet. The room was filled with the silence of embarrassment for what must have seemed a lengthy period, because they understood without being told what lesson was being taught them.

Every worthy Jewish home contained a water jar and towel, with either a servant girl or a member of the family standing by to wash the guests' feet. It was a practical courtesy observed throughout a land noted for its dusty roads where the inhabitants wore open sandals. Not to observe this pleasant custom was considered ill-mannered in the extreme, and the disciples remembered the occasion when such discourtesy had been shown towards Jesus. He had been, surprisingly, invited to the house of Simon the Pharisee. During the meal an uninvited guest entered — an occurrence not uncommon in those days — and stood at Jesus' feet. She was a noted sinful woman who, to the consternation of all present except the chief guest, began bathing his feet with her tears of repentance, and anointing them with very expensive ointment.

Simon and his friends were appalled by the presence of such a woman and of Jesus' acceptance of her, but he used the occasion to convey his teaching: 'Simon, seest thou this woman? I entered into thine house, thou gavest me no water for my feet: but she hath washed my feet with tears, and wiped them with the hairs of her head. Thou gavest me no kiss: but this woman since the time I came in hath not ceased to kiss my feet. My head with oil thou didst not anoint: but this woman hath anointed my feet with ointment. Wherefore I say unto thee, Her sins, which are many, are forgiven; for she hath loved much: but to whom little is forgiven, the same loveth little' (Luke 7:44-47). Jesus then turned to the woman, with the full weight of divine authority, assuring her of forgiveness — an act which produced the expected hostility from the watching guests.

In the upper room, the twelve were distinctly uncomfortable as they watched Jesus performing the function of, and dressed as, a common slave. Twenty-six grimy feet had entered the room after a two-mile walk, but in the absence of the owner of the house or a member of his family to carry out the task, not one of Jesus' guests had volunteered to perform the menial role in bathing the feet of the Master and his friends. Each had been aware of the custom, knew what had to be done and must have felt awkward leaving the jar and towel in their position by the door, but pride had prevented them from offering their services. They were capable of desiring greatness, but not at the expense of a loss of pride.

They felt ashamed, so much so that when Jesus reached Peter's feet and began washing them the latter's embarrassment could not be retained in silence any longer. Echoing the sentiments of all his colleagues, except, one assumes, Judas, Peter exclaimed, 'Lord, dost thou wash *my* feet?' Even then there appeared to be a conflict of interests between the embarrassment at seeing so great a figure humbled before him and the painful process of a conscience pricked and a pride rebuked. However, from what Jesus said it was plain that the ordinary courtesies of hospitality were only one aspect of this unusual act, not the main reason for it: 'If I then, your Lord and Master, have washed your feet; ye also ought to wash one another's feet. For I have given you an example, that ye should do as I have done to you' (John 13:14-15).

There was another factor, one which Peter appeared not to notice: 'What I do thou knowest not now, but thou shalt know hereafter.' This slight insight into the mysteries being unfolded in the upper room stirred Peter's pride still further as he insisted, 'Thou shalt never wash *my* feet,' and there was no doubt that once again, as on so many other occasions, he was reflecting the views of the others. But he heard his Lord say, 'If I wash thee not, thou hast no part with me.'

It is doubtful whether Peter would have understood the significance of Jesus' words even had he contemplated them — that is, not until the Day of Pentecost when he was under the anointing of the Spirit (Acts 2:38) — but in the upper room, with the childlike and attractive impetuosity for which the apostle is renowned, he gave full vent to his devotion to his Master: 'Lord, not my feet only, but also my hands and my head,' to which Jesus replied, 'He that is washed needeth not save to wash his feet, but is clean every whit: and ye are clean, but not all' (John 13:9-10).

Again, Peter appeared to overlook the aside, a reference to Judas, as he discovered that his love for his Lord truly far outweighed his pride, although as subsequent events were to show, there was still much of the latter remaining (Matt. 26:33).

The sight of Jesus removing his clothing and appearing before the apostles as a slave should have provided them, had they been capable of receiving it at the time, with a deeper insight into what the occasion in the upper room signified. Had they the faith to perceive spiritual matters, it would not have taken long to recognize the meaning of the parable Jesus was enacting, the beauty and pathos behind the atonement. There were several remarkable matters the Son of God was conveying to his audience, not one of whom was capable of appreciating any of them at the time.

An act of self-abasement

The first was signified in the act of laying aside that which provides the dignity all men assume is their right, and employing the common towel as an insignia of enslavement. With this gesture, Jesus was re-enacting that 'moment' within the mysteries of eternal glory when a covenant was made between the three persons of the blessed Trinity to secure the redemption of the elect. The Father and the Son spoke one to another, the former expressing his everlasting love for the other in a committed promise: 'Thou art my Son; this day have I begotten thee. Ask of me, and I shall give thee the heathen for thine inheritance, and the uttermost parts of the earth for thy possession' (Ps. 2:7-8). The Son responded with words of absolute devotion, dedication and obedience: 'Lo, I come, in the volume of the book it is written of me, I delight to do thy will, O my God: yea, thy law is within my heart' (Ps. 40:7-8).

Each step of the way, from heaven's glory to earth's gloom, was an experience of deepening humiliation. His seat at the Father's right hand was vacated that he might pass through the angelic hosts (Heb. 2:9), but even being in their company as one 'made so much better than the angels' (Heb. 1:4) entailed the deliberate humbling of himself, for indeed, 'To which of the angels said he at any time, Sit on my right hand, until I make thine enemies thy footstool?' (Heb. 1:13). Then his appearance in the world, with its fallen character manifestly apparent, could bring only grief to his pure heart. His birth was of the lowliest kind, the throne of eternal splendour replaced by a stable's squalor, and his life among men without an abiding resting-place (Luke 9:58).

It might be asked why the Son of God had to stoop so low in order to rescue lost sinners. Why was he obliged to suffer so profoundly before they could be raised to new life in him? The answer is plain. To whatever depths man in his depravity had sunk, the sinless Saviour had to sink lower, whilst remaining sinless, if he was to deal with the cause of man's fall. Superstition and fairy tales would have their heroes waving magic wands from afar to accomplish their aims; the message from heaven faced reality and sent one who was capable of plummeting to the very spot where the victims lay helpless and bound. They who were slaves to sin (John 8:34) required the divine Slave to set them free, and for an eternal rescue to be secured the rescuer had to possess both the experience of the offender and the essence of the Offended One (Heb. 4:15). Only the Son of God's being 'made flesh' (John 1:14) could satisfy the situation.

A slave has nothing of his own

Secondly, if Jesus, standing before his bemused audience in the upper room, stripped of all clothing short of a loincloth, was a visual parable of his substituting eternal glory for human flesh, his kneeling before the feet of sinners was the clearest indication of the divine humility. He who in essence was 'very God of very God', or in the apostle's words 'in the form of God ... equal with God' (Phil. 2:6-11), became a slave, having divested himself of personal rights and status in an act of eternal love (John 13:1). The one before whom all heaven bows, the Creator, and the *raison d'être* for everything created (Col. 1:16), was willing to serve rather than be served (Mark 10:45). In fact, not only did Deity become flesh; that flesh also bore all the hallmarks of serfdom in a full surrender to the needs of others.

As for his death, that final Thursday in the upper room, a few hours prior to the blackness of Calvary, provided a further insight into the wonders of the atonement. After seven years of service an Old Testament slave was given the opportunity of being able to confess, 'I love my master, my wife, and my children; I will not go out free' (Exod. 21:5-6). That being so, his ear was bored through with an awl, the mark of a perpetual enslavement. Jesus loved his Father, his covenant 'wife' and children (Mark 3:33-35); he therefore came under the 'awl' of perfect obedience and was nailed to the tree where he hung passively as a committed slave for sinners.

Through the centuries artists, out of respect for their subject, have always depicted the crucified Christ wearing the loincloth although in fact he would have been naked. A slave has no say in the matter, not being in the position of raising an objection, but must submit to the whims and wishes of those who are his masters. So it was at Calvary. Jesus was stripped of his clothing by the Roman centurion and his legionaries. They in turn, in an act of callous obscenity, with the cries and groans of their victims within hearing a few feet away, ignorantly fulfilled scriptural prophecy (Ps. 22:18) by dividing his only belongings among them (John 19:23-24). A slave has no possessions he can call his own. Even the loincloth Jesus wore in the upper room as he bathed the disciples' feet was a towel which belonged to someone else.

He humbled himself voluntarily

There was a third lesson being taught the twelve that evening: not only the Son of God surrendering himself as a slave, but that slave's abnegation. Before Jewish contempt and abuse Jesus 'reviled not again' (1 Peter 2:23); at the mercy of Roman violence he 'gave ... no answer' (John 19:9); under the scourging he submitted without reserve and when led to Golgotha was 'as a lamb to the slaughter' (Isa. 53:7). Upon the cross he hung naked and bleeding, with nothing to call his own, except his pure love for the Father, a dignity in suffering unmatched by any other and an engrossing love even for those who had crucified him.

The fulfilment of prophecy

Yet Jesus was aware of his predicament. From childhood he had known Psalm 22, a Messianic psalm he had learned by heart, and what better place to recite its graphic poetry within the secret recesses of his soul, than when hanging from the tree destined for him? Jesus, devoid of self-interest ('I am poured out like water'), his body twisted in its agony ('All my bones are out of joint'), in possession of a broken heart ('My heart is like wax; it is melted in the midst of my bowels') and drained of all strength ('My strength is dried up like a potsherd') recognized that he was fulfilling prophecy (Ps. 22:14-15).

His physical condition and torment of soul as he bore the blazing wrath of divine displeasure produced in him great anguish: 'I am a worm, and no man; a reproach of men, and despised of the people' (Ps. 22:6). He heard the raucous laughter and abusive words, but the blasphemy behind them would have hurt even more: 'He trusted on the Lord that he would deliver him: let him deliver him, seeing he delighted in him' (Ps. 22:8). He saw his clothing being shared out among the Roman soldiers ('They part my garments among them, and cast lots upon my vesture', Ps. 22:18), and yet forgave them unreservedly (Luke 23:34). His was a complete isolation on the cross unequalled by any other experience known outside of hell ('Be not far from me; for trouble is near; for there is none to help'), without even the consolation of paternal succour ('My God, my God, why hast thou forsaken me?'), for he was the Master making atonement for his subjects, the Slave ministering to the enslaved (Ps. 22:1-8).

Jesus announces his forthcoming betrayal

The washing of the feet having been accomplished and the embarrassment shared by the apostles somewhat abated, Jesus dressed again and returned to the table for the passover meal. However, if his guests thought the evening would continue without further interruption they were mistaken. They were soon to discover that their Master had not ceased from shocking them. Suddenly, Jesus interrupted the proceedings with such startling news that the response from his friends was swift: 'Verily I say unto you, that one of you shall betray me' (Matt. 26:21). The statement acted like a bolt from the blue with the word, 'betray', appearing to hang on Jesus' lips. His friends knew from experience that a statement from him beginning, 'Verily I say unto you,' was a solemn one. Nevertheless, they looked at one another with incredulity.

Upon reflection, they must have realized that the antagonism of the religious parliament (the Sanhedrin) towards Jesus had sharpened since the previous Sunday. Then Jesus' action in riding on a donkey into Jerusalem at the head of multitudes shouting excitedly, 'Hosanna to the son of David!', had deeply disturbed the chief priests (Matt. 21:8-15). The city had not seen anything like it before. The curious city-dwellers flocked to the temple area to see for themselves what the excitement was about. Thus two huge milling crowds converged, with the figure of Jesus somewhere in the middle, and a carpet of palms paving his way. The viewing priests were obliged to remember the prophet's words: 'Rejoice greatly, O daughter of Zion; shout, O daughter of Jerusalem: behold, thy King cometh unto thee: he is just, and having salvation; lowly, and riding upon an ass, and upon a colt the foal of an ass' (Zech. 9:9). It was clear Jesus was a marked man from then on, that the Sanhedrin would leave no stone unturned to rid themselves of him, and would have done so that day but for the ecstatic crowds (Matt. 21:45-46). What they required was a 'mole' among the apostles to keep them informed of Jesus' whereabouts in readiness for the suitable moment for an arrest.

Something of the gloom hovering over Jerusalem had entered the room. Each conscience, bar one, was visibly stirred. The sinner's conscience is a strange and mysterious instrument, and the closer to Jesus it lingers the more sensitive it becomes. Around the table reverberated the simple challenge: 'Lord, is it I?' (Matt. 26:22). Even though the question was asked by eleven innocent men, such is the depravity of human nature that they felt obliged to ask it. They knew Jesus understood they were not guilty of betraying him to the authorities, yet had they not 'betrayed' him with every sinful act upon each day they had known him?

The question hung in the air. Jesus continued to apply pressure to the one conscience that mattered that evening. If only the culprit would admit his guilt! To all present he said, 'He that dippeth his hand with me in the dish, the same shall betray me' (Matt. 26:23). So the betrayer was actually in the room, within nudging distance. One could have cut the atmosphere with a knife. All thirteen hands were at that moment hovering around the very large dish which stood in the centre of the table, but one of them belonged to an enemy. They could scarcely comprehend what they were hearing, so fearful was the suggestion. Peter, reclining near his friend John, suggested he should ask Jesus who the betrayer was. John, so close to Jesus his head could touch his chest, did as Peter requested. However, Jesus did not answer directly. Instead he whispered to John that the betrayer was about to receive a morsel from him. John and Peter watched carefully as Jesus' hand reached into the dish. Judas! (John 13:23-26).

The painful enquiries, 'Lord is it I?', having lapsed into a stunned silence, the twelve quickly discovered Jesus had not completed his examination. He still desired the offender to admit his guilt, and gave him another opportunity for doing so. This time there could be no possibility of underestimating the gravity of the crime committed against the Son of God: 'The Son of man goeth as it is written of him: but woe unto that man by whom the Son of man is betrayed! It had been good for that man if he had not been born' (Matt. 26:24). If the culprit refused to confess at that point and, weeping, beg for divine mercy, the hardness of his heart would forbid redemption or hope of any kind.

One would have thought the solemnity of the proceedings might have hushed and humbled pride, and caused each of the twelve to search his heart. But no! The eleven innocent of the charge began to make the most noise, even holding a discussion among themselves as to which of them was guilty of the heinous offence. In fact, so strenuously did they debate the issue that pride leapt high and thoughts of personal accountability were conveniently forgotten. They even pursued the well-worn notion that one was greater than another. On such an evening, with Calvary not far away, Jesus must have wearied of their arguing and strife (Luke 22:23-27).

It was probably during the wrangling that the culprit, known to his Master all along, revealed himself. The eleven were so engrossed with gaining points over the others that they failed to see Judas leave his position at the table (surely, as far removed from Jesus as possible) and walk quietly towards him. His question, no doubt whispered, was not contrite, for there was no spirit of repentance behind it. In fact, it was an empty echo of what had already been asked, as if mocking the Saviour. Without doubt Satan was in that room (John 13:2,27). One can imagine Judas wrily grinning when he asked, 'Master, is it I?' (Matt. 26:25). Jesus agreed that it was, and shortly afterwards suggested that what he had to do should be accomplished without delay. Of the rest, all but Peter and John were ignorant of what Jesus meant and assumed Judas had to leave their company on business connected with his task as the group's treasurer (John 13:27-30). They little realized the nature of the business, or the circumstances under which they would next see him.

The mystery of Judas

It was night in more ways than one (John 13:30). What Judas' feelings were when he left the room would have been unfathomable,

even if they were known. He would not have been able to untangle
them himself, such was his unique role in the drama unfolding
around him. No one this side of eternity is capable of entering into
the three mysteries of which he was a central figure.

The first was the stated fact that *Jesus had chosen him to be an
apostle*, despite knowing him to be 'a devil' (John 6:70). Jesus'
action was not philanthropic, the desire that Judas' nature might
change merely by being in his company, for Judas could have been
converted without being made an apostle. Besides, Jesus was not a
pragmatist, but always acted along absolute lines provided by his
Father. Indeed, with noticeable deliberation he stated to his guests
that night in the upper room, 'I know whom I have chosen: but that
the scripture may be fulfilled, He that eateth bread with me hath
lifted up his heel against me' (John 13:18).

There is no doubt Judas was called to be an apostle to fulfil both
the will of the triune God and the Scriptures which reveal what that
will is. As far as Judas was concerned, 'He it was that should betray
him' (John 6:71), appointed to do so from eternity, and thus to fulfil
scriptural prophecy: 'What are these wounds in thine hands? Then
he shall answer, Those with which I was wounded in the house of
my friends' (Zech. 13:6). In other words, there is only one way in
which Judas' function as the betrayer can be understood, and the
depth of the mystery is so awe-inspiring that man cannot begin to
comprehend it. He was elected from eternity for the betrayal.

Then there is the mystery of *Judas' relationship to Satan*. Even
whilst being among the other apostles he was still a 'devil'; he was
one before Jesus set eyes upon him, and he remained one to the end
(Matt. 27:5). The Saviour of sinners and Lord of all prayed for Peter
when Satan was 'sifting' him (Luke 22:31-32), but we do not read
that Jesus prayed for Judas. He was left to Satan because he
belonged to him, numbered among the 'natural brute beasts, made
to be taken and destroyed' (2 Peter 2:12.) He was an open door
through which Satan entered at will, a darkened soul who in a
particular way was his representative as well as his child. When
Satan, who himself is always under the direct control of God (Job
1:12), desired the betrayal of Christ he 'put into the heart of Judas

Iscariot, Simon's son, to betray him' (John 13:2) and the betrayer carried out the satanic wishes because his devilish master had 'entered' him (Luke 22:3). Judas was Satan's man for the hour.

The third mystery concerns *Judas as a man*. History knows of no more tragic figure, one who walked with God manifest in flesh yet was driven to betray him. What was said to John the Baptist by Jesus could equally have been said to Judas: 'The blind receive their sight, and the lame walk, the lepers are cleansed, and the deaf hear, the dead are raised up, and the poor have the gospel preached to them' (Matt. 11:5). But unlike John, Judas saw it all at first hand, and therefore was without excuse for his treachery. He had been present at the most dramatic occasions in the ministry of Jesus as well as the tenderest, from the stilling of the storm upon Galilee's lake (Matt. 8:23-27) to the embracing of infants brought to Jesus for blessing (Luke 18:15). But, like every apostate, he found himself part of Christ's church, mingling freely with those who loved the Saviour, yet realizing deep within himself his inability to share their devotion. He possessed the true religion without the grace to accompany it, being as much a thief at the end as at the beginning; he walked with Christ without submitting to him and throughout this period felt the innate compulsion to oppose the Son of God on the one hand (John 12:4-8), and even to do him harm on the other. However, had Judas not betrayed Jesus, had he lived the life-span of his fellow apostles, sooner or later he would have forsaken the group and joined those with whom he felt more at ease — the irreligious. For, we are told of apostates, 'if they shall fall away', it is impossible 'to renew them again unto repentance; seeing they crucify to themselves the Son of God afresh, and put him to an open shame' (Heb. 6:6).

It has been suggested by many that the betrayal was the result of Judas' disillusionment about Jesus, because he failed to live up to the national expectation of the Messiah — namely, that upon arrival in Israel he would liberate his people from the bondage of the Roman occupation. It is argued that, in betraying the Lord, Judas sought to force him to raise the expected army and claim his throne.

Certainly, such teaching circulated throughout Israel, from the Sanhedrin to the disciples (Acts 1:6), but this view is hardly correct for there was much more to the Judas enigma than it suggests. Faced as he was with the evidence of Christ's deity, he was not likely to try to force Jesus into any situation, knowing the futility of doing so. Judas had known exactly what he was doing when he first approached the Sanhedrin a short while before to negotiate the betrayal of the Lord (Luke 22:1-6). The secrecy behind his clandestine meeting with the priests would have been carefully thought out as well as meticulously planned. It was a daring thing to do, for despite his willingness to betray Jesus, Caiaphas and the council had nothing but contempt for Judas as a noted member of Jesus' most intimate group. The Sanhedrin, who were capable of arranging Jesus' death, would have no problem in disposing of Judas once his information had been divulged. The risk was immense, but it reveals the strong compulsion he felt from Satan's influence to continue in his wickedness despite the possible outcome.

The Sanhedrin was in a quandary: having agreed in council that Jesus should be arrested and killed, they realized that such an extreme action could not be carried out without the possibility of a popular revolt. They had witnessed the clamour and excitement as their quarry entered Jerusalem a few days earlier, and knew his popularity was likely to mark their downfall if it was thought Jesus was in any way threatened by them. Thus, when Judas offered his services Caiaphas and his fellow priests rejoiced that their plan could be brought to fruition without openly involving them. As a result they gave him a paltry thirty pieces of silver, the price paid to the owner of a slave gored by an ox (Exod. 21:32). It was a studied insult both to Jesus and to Judas, and the latter must have objected when he was offered so little for such a valuable item of news, but the bargain having been struck, there was nothing he could do. Once Jesus' whereabouts had been revealed, Judas' usefulness was over and he would have been quickly paid off and shown the door.

The traitor's doom

As Judas made his way from the upper room through the darkness to his rendezvous with treachery, Jesus' alarming warning was still reverberating around his conscience: 'The Son of man goeth as it is written of him: but woe unto that man by whom the Son of man is betrayed! It had been good for that man if he had not been born' (Matt. 26:24). Such words, spoken with the sobriety of the Judge, did not cause Judas to falter; the satanic compulsion was by this time too intense. He had an appointment with destiny and was obliged to keep it, his betrayal as certain to be carried out as the crucifixion of the one he betrayed.

With his valuable information, Judas headed towards the ap-pointed meeting-place as quickly as he could to earn his wages of a few silver coins (Matt. 26:15). He must have guessed the transaction could only harm him, as no one could seek to destroy the Son of God and hope to escape a revenging Providence. The moment arrived within hours.

Everyone is by nature the devil's child (Eph. 2:1-3), swayed by satanic influences, and only the power of Christ's atoning blood can liberate us (Col. 1:13). However, there are some within Satan's family for whom 'the prince' has a special interest. Judas was one of them, and tragedy is the only possible outcome of such an encounter (John 14:30). The victim is first overshadowed, then filled with the tormentor's evil intentions (John 13:2), and finally enveloped like a trapped fly entangled on a spider's web. Drawn into the darkest recesses of Satan's embrace, he slowly succumbs to his master's every whim, self-control gone.

The experience may not last long. Satan is a fickle lover; his usefulness over, the victim is ignominiously discarded in preference for someone else. He has escaped, but is not free, for no one emerging from the blackness of such a shadow can claim liberty as his reward. The satanic lordship over him will have left an indelible mark, evil having permeated every nook and cranny of his life, and he awakes from the horror realizing he is left eternally destitute, degraded and destroyed (2 Peter 2:12).

Judas was no exception. The man who had bargained for Christ's life with such panache and cunning, a willing tool in the hands of destructive forces, had also been in possession of the assured confidence provided by Satan's approval. Even betraying the Son of God with a kiss had not caused Judas concern, but now suddenly he felt desolate (Ps. 69:25). No longer was he bolstered by an apparent invincibility; he was isolated with only his conscience for company. Satan had flung him to one side, his work completed; it was all over in more ways than one.

All that was left was the horrific realization of what he had done, an account his conscience recalled repeatedly to his tormented mind. God the Son, by whom and for whom the entire universe had been created (Col. 1:15-19), the daily delight of the Father, in whose presence he had throughout eternity rejoiced always before him (Prov. 8:30), had been betrayed by a mere mortal he had befriended (Zech. 13:6). Had Judas examined the annals of history, even searched the records of eternal ages past, would he have discovered a crime more heinous? Only one perhaps stood any chance of being its equal — that 'moment' in heaven prior to the creation when the devil, who later caused the fall of man in the garden of Eden (Gen. 3), had sought God's throne and had been cast out with the angels who fell with him (Isa. 14:12-15).

Christ was now safely in the hands of the authorities, and in a short while would be crucified, but there was nothing Judas could do to alleviate the situation. It was too late. His desolation was severe (Acts 1:20), his isolation complete; he was without support and sympathy from anyone in heaven or upon the earth. Nevertheless his remorse had to be expressed, someone, however hateful of him, must hear it.

It was a poor attempt, but all that Judas could do, when he returned to the temple with the thirty coins. He knew where, of all places, the priests would be. He burst in upon them, and cried out his guilt, throwing his paltry payment on the floor. Their indifference to his plight and pain must have been expected, but served to underline the fact that he was bereft of all help and hope. Suicide was the only 'comfort' he could find (Matt. 27:3-5), but for the 'son of perdition' any relief would have been short-lived (John 17:12).

Judas had gone, but the coins remained, and the priests were more concerned with them than with him. Less defiled in God's sight than the supposed custodians of temple worship, the thirty pieces were not permitted a place in the sacred treasury since they were 'the price of blood', as if they had paid themselves into Judas' hand! Instead, with an insult to the Gentile races, a cemetery was bought for them with the 'blood money' (Matt. 27:6-10). It was appropriate that such a man should be remembered by a cemetery (Acts 1:18-19), and his treachery foretold by a godly prophet (Zech. 11:12-13).

However, at the point we have reached in our study, Judas' tragic end had yet to take place. In the meantime, the upper room was filled with an atmosphere of anticipation and foreboding.

2.
The impending departure

What had begun as an evening of quiet fellowship among friends, the celebration of passover, had turned into one of discomfort and distress for the apostles as they were made to realize the significance of the occasion. They had been acutely embarrassed by Jesus' gracious display in washing their feet and alarmed by the sudden announcement of intended betrayal, and by this time they wondered what was going to confront them next.

They were not to wait long. The eleven were engrossed in the meal, when Jesus suddenly broke into the hubbub of general conversation with fresh information: 'I have desired to eat this passover with you before I suffer,' and as they pondered the reference to his suffering, he continued, 'I will not any more eat..., until it be fulfilled in the kingdom of God' (Luke 22:15,16). He had spoken of his suffering before, although the information never appeared to be understood (Matt. 16:21-22), but now the time had arrived for it to take place. Jesus was leaving them, and the meal would be their last together.

The reaction of the disciples

Whether his imminent suffering weighed more heavily upon them than his intended departure is to be doubted, but the eleven friends were filled with consternation as the shock waves swept over them.

They had heard him speak like this before (John 13:33). They had heard him say his time in the world would be brief and 'Then I go unto him that sent me,' but in the throes of the controversy which surrounded that statement they had not questioned him further. However, they remembered him saying to his audience at the time that they would look for him in vain, and in any case, would be incapable of accompanying him (John 7:33-34). In fact the world would be glad, would even 'rejoice', to see the back of him (John 16:20).

The sad anticipated moment had finally arrived. Jesus and his friends were shortly to part company, but they were not to grieve. Their sorrow would turn to joy! (John 16:22). Although they could not accompany him on the final stages of his lonely mission, the supreme and ultimate sacrifice of himself for sinners (John 13:31-35), they would see him again. Beyond the anguish, via the empty tomb, lay the exaltation to the highest pinnacle of adoration and praise (Phil. 2:9-10).

Instead of rejoicing, the bewildered men were caught between their desire to be with him and the latent half-belief that had dogged their understanding throughout their time with Jesus. Once more an air of unease descended upon the room as their lack of faith was exposed, for what value had they placed upon Jesus' teaching when after three years they still failed to recognize his deity and embrace it as a glorious reality? They were made aware that, with their Master's imminent departure, they were at heart still rooted in earth and not in heaven (Phil. 3:20).

Many years later, John the apostle looked back in retrospect at their years with the Master and was able to state categorically under the anointing of the Holy Spirit , 'The life was manifested, and we have seen it, and bear witness, and show unto you that eternal life, which was with the Father, and was manifested unto us' (1 John 1:2). At the farewell supper, though, such confidence was noticeably absent among the apostles.

It was too much for Peter. The thought of Jesus leaving them all produced the immediate response one would have expected from him: his curiosity to know where his Lord was going, coupled with an eagerness to travel with him. Jesus' response to the childlike earnestness appeared a comforting one to Peter at the time — the fact that one day he would indeed follow him — but the significance of Jesus' statement escaped his notice. Later, in conversation beside the Sea of Galilee after the resurrection, the manner in which Peter would 'follow' Jesus was made plain. The Lord spoke mysteriously of the fisherman stretching forth his hands, and of being carried in a direction he would not wish to go — in other words death by crucifixion, although of course for different reasons (John 21:18). But in the meantime, a shameful denial of his Lord would precede the eventual martyrdom (John 13:36,38). The Son of God prefers reality to dreams!

To alleviate the sadness his words had caused, Jesus consoled his friends still further. Not only was he returning to the Father in a short while, but eventually they would be joining him. In fact, he was going to prepare a place for them and one day they would all be reunited (John 14:1-3). His teaching should have been familiar to them, and he said so: 'And whither I go ye know, and the way ye know.' After all, not long before, Jesus had provided them with a graphic picture of what it would be like on that momentous day when 'the Son of man shall come in his glory'. Mankind will be separated into two camps, the unsaved ('goats') and the redeemed ('sheep'), and the latter will be consoled with the most beautiful expression of eternal love they could hear: 'Come, ye blessed of my Father, inherit the kingdom prepared for you from the foundation of the world' (Matt. 25:31-34).

It was not only Peter who was puzzled, John noticed. Thomas and Philip were too, or perhaps they were just more prepared than the rest to confess their confusion openly (John 14:5-10). Men whose major occupation throughout their adult lives had been fishing were finding they were in far deeper waters now and unable to cope. Thomas particularly, intensely practical, found it perplexing having to grapple with abstract concepts. Like the majority of believers since, he found it easier to relate to his Lord's death than to his resurrection and ascension to glory (John 20:26-28): 'Lord, we know not whither thou goest, and how can we know the way?'

How strange that Thomas should call him Lord, yet did not know the ultimate destination, or the way to it! When Jesus reminded him in effect that he was Lord of all, the signpost, the road to the Father and the reason for travelling on it, he lapsed into silence, probably still as mystified as before the question was asked (John 14:5-7).

Philip, on the other hand, reflected a different personality — excitable, and with more zeal than understanding. Three years earlier, in Galilee, when Jesus called him to be a disciple, Philip quickly looked for his friend Nathanael (Bartholomew) exclaiming excitedly, 'We have found him, of whom Moses in the law, and the prophets did write, Jesus of Nazareth, the son of Joseph' (John 1:45). To his astonishment Nathanael was unimpressed, without even bothering to see for himself, not believing that any 'good thing' could spring from the insignificant town of Nazareth. Why, it was not even mentioned in his Bible!

Besides, being more phlegmatic than Philip and certainly more familiar with biblical truth, Nathanael knew that according to the prophet Micah the Messiah was due to appear in the south of the country, Judah. Nazareth was in the north. Philip was so eager that he had failed to consider the prophecy, where in a beautiful passage Micah addresses 'Bethlehem Ephratah' (Ephrath being the original name, Gen. 35:19) as the place whence the 'ruler in Israel' would arise (5:2). In any case, surely Matthew would have told Philip during their days together of the experience of the wise men thirty years or so earlier (Matt. 2).

Philip's zeal persisted but he was still prone, like many today, to substitute subjective feelings for objective truth. If only Jesus would enable them to see the Father about whom he had spoken so frequently, how much easier it would be to believe! He had spent years with Jesus, but had failed to appreciate the fundamental and remarkable truth his Lord put to him that evening that 'He that hath seen me hath seen the Father' (John 14:8-9). But Philip was still puzzled, and he would not be the last in subsequent history, as he grappled with the unique revelation relating to the two natures of Christ. Within the confines of the upper room conversing with Philip and the rest was the Son of God/Son of man (Dan. 7:13-14), the God-man, who in essence is one with the Father and yet equally one with man in every experience known to him except that of natural depravity (Heb. 4:15).

To gaze at Christ, then, is to gaze at God himself in his perfect righteousness, beauty and grace. At the same time, union with the Son grants a true knowledge of the majestic being of God the Father — to clutch the hem of ultimate mystery. Christ is the Word 'made flesh' who was 'with God', 'set up from everlasting, from the beginning, or ever the earth was' (Prov. 8:23). In short, he 'was God' (John 1:1,14). As God the Son he descended to earth from glory, as a word issues from a mouth, revealing and communicating 'secrets' from deep within the counsels of the Godhead (Dan. 2:47). He, and he only, it is imperative to emphasize in a multi-faith society, is capable of doing so.

He has broken perfection's 'seals' (seven in all, Rev. 5) unfolding what thoughts and feelings of Deity it is his will to communicate, so that to Christ mankind must go if it wishes to discover what they are. To 'know' him is to 'know' the Father, and to hear him is to hear the Father. Likewise to have read about his miraculous powers, or to have witnessed them in the regenerating energies of the Spirit, is to have touched the sovereign majesty of God himself (John 14:10-11). As John the apostle was later to testify, 'We beheld his glory, the glory as of the only begotten of the Father, full of grace and truth' (John 1:14).

Undoubtedly, Philip was still bewildered, but had he thought about it would have remembered Jesus' earlier forthright statement: 'I and my Father are one' (John 10:30). In any case, had he examined his Bible more thoroughly he would have read Isaiah's mysterious words relating to the coming Prince of Peace, that he is 'Wonderful, Counsellor, the mighty God, the everlasting Father' — all in one (Isa. 9:6).

Years later another apostle, who was not present at the farewell supper, climaxed one of his letters with a doxology reminiscent of that occasion when he described Jesus in terms fitting only for deity (1 Tim. 6:15-16). In it the Old and New Testaments meet in God the Son, glorified as 'the blessed and only Potentate [Deut. 6:4], the

King of kings [Dan. 2:37], and Lord of lords [Ps. 136:3]; who only
hath immortality [Dan. 4:34], dwelling in the light which no man
can approach unto [Exod. 40:35], whom no man hath seen, nor can
see [Deut. 4:12]: to whom be honour and power everlasting [1 Chron.
29:10-13].'

The Lord's Supper

There was a further surprise awaiting the eleven. As they ate the
passover meal, Jesus introduced what has since become known as
the Lord's Supper. A silence descended upon the gathering as the
friends watched him solemnly pick a piece of unleavened bread
from a plate close at hand, over which he offered a prayer of thanksgiving. He then broke the slice of bread into the appropriate pieces
before passing them around the table to his friends, each of whom
fixed his attention upon Jesus as he spoke the words so familiar to
succeeding generations of his followers: 'Take, eat: this is my body'
(Matt. 26:26), and then added, as Paul was informed, 'which is
broken for you; this do in remembrance of me' (1 Cor. 11:24).

Within that brief moment in which three simple actions took
place, the short prayer, the swift snapping of the crisp bread and its
distribution, three truths were revealed.

The prayer

First was the prayer of blessing. Although its contents are not
known, one can hazard an intelligent guess that it contained the
recognition of how crucial was the moment. Jesus knew 'his hour
was come' (John 13:1), that the atoning sacrifice he had to endure
was near. It was therefore fitting to anticipate with thanksgiving
what the consequences were to be for sinners — not only for his
friends gathered around the table at that moment, but for an innumerable company from 'all nations, and kindreds, and people,
and tongues' (Rev. 7:9). Within hours the gates of heaven would be
flung wide open for all believers, the hope of generations realized.
The stillness within the room, broken only by the sound of Jesus'

voice, was a moving moment: heaven's High Priest seeking blessing from the Father upon the symbol of the sacrifice he had been
appointed to make.

The bread

The prayer over, Jesus looked at the sacrificial symbol (and it was
no more than that) in the palm of his hand. Bread has always been
the staff of life since very early times, that which not only prevents
hunger but nourishes the body, providing it with the necessary
strength and vigour (Lev. 26:26). The peasant toiled long and hard
that he might feed his family with enough for each day, as God
promised Adam following the Fall: 'In the sweat of thy face shalt
thou eat bread' (Gen. 3:19).

As Jesus stared at the slice in front of him, he saw beyond its
outward appearance to a spiritual significance. Was not its presence
on the table due to the Creator whose hand now held it (Col. 1:16),
and did not the grain 'fall into the ground and die' (John 12:24)
before producing the wheat from which the bread came? Jesus, the
'true bread' who gives life to the world (John 6:32-33), sprang as the
choicest of the 'wheat' from the 'dry ground' of Nazareth (Isa.
53:2). His astonishing statement, 'I am the bread of life: he that
cometh to me shall never hunger' (John 6:31-35), has been relevant
in every generation since. No corner of the globe is excluded from
the sound of his voice or from the generous appeal which the passage
of time cannot make null and void. For those who desire everlasting
life, it is imperative that their souls feed on such life-giving susten-
ance (John 6:51).

Then again, the bread over which Jesus had prayed was
unleavened. Unlike the housewives of most nations, from earliest
times Jewish women baked their bread without leaven mixed with
the dough (Gen. 19:3), for leaven, being sour, possesses the element
of corruption (Matt. 16:6). Conversely, for the Jew unleavened
bread symbolized purity and life. When God instructed Moses to
establish the first passover feast (Exod.12), not only were the people
to shelter from the avenging angel under the sprinkled sacrificial
blood of an unblemished lamb; they were to eat the passover meal

'roast with fire, *and unleavened bread*; and with bitter herbs' (Exod. 12:8). Purity was the word: the appeasing blood, the 'uncorrupted' bread and the purifying fires which engulfed the sacrificial offerings. Later, as Deuteronomy teaches us, the week following the passover was entitled 'the feast of unleavened bread', for that was what the Israelites were commanded to eat as a symbol of the purification fulfilled in Christ (Deut. 16:16).

But Jesus not only gave thanks for the bread, *he broke it into pieces,* and as he did so his words, 'Take eat, this is my body' (Matt. 26:26), spoken with such solemnity, must have had a profound effect upon the eleven. They were beginning to understand as far as they were able, and probably for the first time, what he had meant earlier in the evening when speaking of his imminent departure. He too lay passively as it were upon a hand, the hand of the Father who orders all events in accordance with his will and purpose (Eph. 1:11), and at the appointed time the hand would close into a fist and tighten its grip. When it opened again the pure Son of God would lie broken upon it, experiencing the agony portrayed in the Messianic psalm mentioned earlier: 'I am poured out like water, and all my bones are out of joint: my heart is like wax; it is melted in the midst of my bowels' (Ps. 22:14). Like the sacrificial lambs (Exod. 12:46), although 'out of joint' not one bone of his would be broken (John 19:36).

The distribution of the bread

Jesus' third act, following the prayer and the breaking of the bread, was the distribution of its pieces. As he passed the plate around to the eleven, he encouraged each one by expressing his love for them. He had wanted them all to meet together because it was to be literally his last supper, 'until it be fulfilled in the kingdom of God' (Luke 22:15-16). His words proved a great comfort. How honoured they felt in having been chosen as his apostles and friends! They were aware of their background, that of very ordinary men drawn mainly from the lower social strata, yet the Son of God had 'desired' to be their companion throughout his ministry in Israel, and even during this period of intense pressure.

They were also consoled, and deeply moved, in knowing their Lord would shortly suffer and die — for *them*. Theological issues were beyond their grasp at this time, but Jesus could not have expressed the gracious motivation behind his sacrifice more clearly than when, earlier in the evening, he had stated simply, 'Greater love hath no man than this, that a man lay down his life for his friends' (John 15:13). This is the definitive explanation of the meaning of love. Many years later, John supplied another: 'Herein is love, not that we loved God, but that he loved us, and sent his Son to be the propitiation for our sins' (1 John 4:10).

True love is like that: vulnerable and sensitive, risking rebuttal, it has to express itself. Heaven's grace made the initial advances towards mankind (John 3:16). Sadly, like most disciples since, they wanted something *from* him, but his only desire was to reveal his love *for* them, and seek a response, however feeble (John 21:15-17). The Son of God loved them, and each child of his since (John 17), despite their sinfulness and failings. Within hours they would forsake him when he needed them most (Matt. 26:56) and Peter would deny that he even knew him (Luke 22:55-62). Then Thomas would doubt his resurrection (John 20:26-29). Yet he still loved them. Unbelievers, instead of noting how few are Christ's followers, should marvel that there are any at all. Left to our own devices we would all have 'forsaken him and fled', but divine love has an irresistible drawing power (Hosea 11:1-4). The existence of Christianity is a remarkable miracle, having its roots in the sheer grace of a loving God.

Something else they would have noticed: Jesus' care for each individual around the table. They all shared equally in the fellowship. No one was overlooked, whatever his failings or however few his talents. Each took his piece of bread in the knowledge that the Saviour loved him deeply on a personal level. There were no favourites. As if to emphasize this, he assured them that he would not call them servants any more, 'for the servant knoweth not what his lord doeth', but friends. What the Father had told him he had revealed to them (John 15:15). What had he 'heard' his Father say? That these were the men especially chosen from the world to be his apostles (John 15:19), who were to receive the truth to which he bore testimony (John 18:37) by being indwelt by God the Spirit (John 16:13). Likewise, for these few, as well as for his flock as a whole, he promised glory as their destination in the bliss of a divine and everlasting love (John 17:24).

The wine

The eleven having eaten their share of the bread, Jesus spent a moment in prayer before passing the wine to them in turn. They looked at him with intensity as he spoke the words no one present could misunderstand: 'Drink ye all of it; for this is my blood of the new testament, which is shed for many for the remission of sins.' Again, his love shone through to them when he continued, 'But I say unto you, I will not drink henceforth of this fruit of the vine, until that day when I drink it new with you in my Father's kingdom' (Matt. 26:27-29).

The final farewells of a man on the eve of his execution are always harrowing and deeply moving to all present, but when that person was Jesus, the effect must have been almost unbearable. No one, surely, would have moved; all would have been riveted to his every act and word. There was no disputing his message, one which every Jew would understand.

First he was directing their attention to *the preciousness of blood,* even animal blood. It travels through the veins providing the body with its life, 'for the life of the flesh is in the blood' (Lev. 17:11), as all creation knows. In Old Testament times the Creator placed such value upon animal blood, strictly forbidding the drinking of it (1 Sam. 14:34), that the slaughter of any animal was considered a sacrificial act, because its blood represented a God-given life. It was either sprinkled upon the altar (Lev. 1:5), or poured out to God on the ground and reverently covered (Deut. 12:24).

How much more valuable then is human blood, a fact underlined by God in the post-diluvian world: 'Whoso sheddeth man's blood, by man shall his blood be shed, for in the image of God made he man' (Gen. 9:6). Human blood is precious, because it is the essence of the life of one made in the Creator's image for worship and devoted service (Deut. 6:5). The fall of man marred that beautiful reflection, but did not destroy it; therefore the killing of another human being is said to pollute the land (Num. 35:33-34), from where the blood of the victim cries out to God (Gen. 4:10).

The other matter which Jesus wished to stress was that if human and animal blood is so valuable, what can be said of *the blood of Christ*? No more precious commodity can there be than that which flowed through the veins of the Word made flesh. It is indeed 'without blemish and without spot' (1 Peter 1:19), and fulfilled the scriptural directive: 'I have given it to you upon the altar to make atonement for your souls, for it is the blood that maketh an atonement for the soul' (Lev. 17:11). They had watched him pour the wine into the cup, and perhaps had remembered the story of Jacob's reaction to being shown Joseph's blood-spattered coat by his brothers. Without being told whose blood it was (goat's blood as it happened) and where it had come from, Jacob instinctively assumed that 'An evil beast hath devoured him; Joseph is without doubt rent in pieces' (Gen. 37:33). Jacob's reaction was a typically Jewish one, in which blood signified, not just death, but one caused by violence.

The eleven listening to Jesus' words would have been in no doubt as to what he meant. He was soon to drink deeply of the cup of suffering from which his life's blood would be poured (Matt. 26:39), the blood with which the everlasting covenant between God and his elect people was signed (Rev. 13:8). Valuable though animal blood is to God, the blood of the sacrificial offerings served only to anticipate the atoning power of the Lamb of God (Rom. 3:25), and was incapable of washing away sin (Heb. 9:12-13). Only at Calvary, the trysting-place where mercy met truth and righteousness kissed peace (Ps. 85:10), could sin ultimately be dealt with. There the broken law was hammered into the cross, whilst the Saviour received the blows of the divine retribution in his own body (Col. 2:14).

The high-priestly prayer

The time spent in the upper room had drawn to a close. If they had been in any doubt at the beginning of the evening, it was now clear that their three-year friendship with him had reached its climax. Still, the sadness of the occasion had been alleviated by the assurance that they were not to be left without comfort. In fact, with their Master's teaching that evening had dawned the truth relating to the continuing ministry of God the Spirit. He would be sent by the Father to console them with his peace and would guide them into the truth which the Son had outlined during his time with them (John 14:26-27). Their need for enlightenment was to be satisfied, their present sorrow turned to joy and their asssurance of the Father's love substantiated (John 16).

If the evening had begun distressfully with the news of the betrayal, it ended in triumphant joy. Just before their departure the Good Shepherd (John 10:11) ministered to his 'little flock' (Luke 12:32) by leading them to the most pleasant of all pastures, the throne of God. As he stood before them with hands outstretched (1 Tim. 2:8) and eyes open and directed towards heaven as was the custom (John 17:1), the disciples believed they were in the presence of the eternal High Priest within the veil (Exod. 28:35). It was an awesome moment, which must have produced in the flock a profound awareness of the divine presence unique even to them after several years of such experiences. If each Christian can be assured of God drawing near to him when he prays (James 4:8), one can only imagine how close they felt to God when the Son spoke to the Father.

In any case, they knew Moses had been physically incapable of entering the tabernacle when the glory of God filled it (Exod. 40:35), and nor could the priests at a later date at the inauguration of the temple worship (1 Kings 8:11), yet they were as close to the glory of God as it was physically possible to be (John 1:14,18). They knew they were standing upon very sacred territory.

The Scriptures are silent about how the eleven friends reacted to hearing Jesus' closing prayer, but there can be no doubt that although they had heard him pray before, on this occasion it was different. They knew they were standing upon the threshold of a new era, when their Lord would be continuing his ministry from within them rather than by their side (John 14:17). Life had not been the same for them since they first met Jesus. Now another dramatic change was about to take place with the crucifixion, resurrection and ascension following swiftly one upon another. As apostles they were to be the custodians of Christ's gospel, and as such part of the foundation upon which the New Testament church would eternally stand (Eph. 2:20-22).

Despite their boastings to the contrary (Matt. 26:33-35), Jesus knew the transitional period was not going to be without its difficulties. With the Shepherd beside them they felt strong and determined, but within hours, as he forewarned them that evening, they would 'be scattered, every man to his own' (John 16:32). They would have to wait some weeks, until the Spirit of Christ came upon them (Acts 2:1-12), before the world would observe that 'Great grace was upon them all' (Acts 4:33).

The impression which lingered for the men who first heard Jesus' prayer in the upper room, as well as for Christians of succeeding generations, was surely one of exhilaration (John 17). Despite the apparent ominous finality of Jesus' opening phrase, 'The hour is come,' the entire prayer was filled with triumphant hope. They who found it so difficult to pray (Luke 11:1), an admission shared by all the children of God, were privileged to be allowed access into the intimate communion between the Father and the Son. Time appeared to stand still as eternity flooded the room, and each disciple lost touch with the feelings of personal grandeur he had revealed earlier in the evening (Luke 22:24). Suddenly, the rivals reclining at the table recognized their abject poverty of spirit as they were confronted with prayer at its most sublime. At last they were united as they listened to the greatest, and undoubtedly the definitive, exposition of the Christian gospel. They probably felt like Moses when confronted with the living God, whose initial reaction was to sink to his knees and worship (Exod. 34:8).

The glory of the Lord

As Jesus proceeded in prayer, they were reminded of three outstanding truths. The first was their Lord's exalted position, his oneness with the Father, clearly demonstrated in his miraculous powers and authoritative statements. In fact, they had been present when the crowds had thrown stones at Jesus in their astonishment at hearing him say, 'Before Abraham was, I am' (John 8:58). The audience had scarcely been able to believe their ears for 'I am' is the sacred name for God, the revelation given to Moses who was instructed to tell the Hebrews in Egypt 'I AM HATH SENT ME UNTO YOU' (Exod. 3:14).

There was no disputing the message Jesus was giving them — namely, that he was God in human form. Now, hearing him in communion with the Father served to substantiate the truth, for his was no ordinary prayer, containing as it did references to eternity unique to his knowledge. Who else but Christ could speak of having shared equally in the glory of God even before the world's creation? (John 17:5). Who else but he could yearn to return to the bosom of the divine love he had experienced before? (John17:24). The elevation of his soul, his divine purity, shone brightly through the intimate expressions of his love for the Father.

Despite the fact that Jesus had yet to arrive at Calvary, such was his determination to do the will of the Father that he spoke as if all had been accomplished: 'I have finished the work which thou gavest me to do' (John 17:4). The divine plan had been fulfilled in all but the experience of its final agony (John 19:30), blessed resurrection and triumphant ascension, and because of this loving obedience the Father had rewarded his Son with ultimate honour.

The first participants in this wonderful prayer heard their Lord's astonishing claim which is unequalled in the recorded utterances of man: 'Thou hast given him power over all flesh' (John 17:2). The apostle Paul echoes this amazing truth in a heart-warming passage: 'And being found in fashion as a man, he humbled himself, and became obedient unto death, even the death of the cross. Wherefore God also hath highly exalted him, and given him a name which is above every name: that at the name of Jesus every knee should bow, of things in heaven, and things in earth; and things under the earth, and that every tongue should confess that Jesus Christ is Lord, to the glory of God the Father' (Phil. 2:8-11).

The revelation of hidden truths

The second aspect of the prayer which must have caused the eleven to wonder, was the height to which Jesus led them when speaking of eternal concepts, all of which he had outlined to them during his ministry from time to time, but now these truths were assembled together, making a humbling impact not only upon those in the upper room, but upon every Christian reader of the seventeenth chapter of John's Gospel since that night.

What Paul was later to call 'the invisible things' (Rom. 1:20) had come upon them. Heaven's refreshing purity filled the room, preventing the fears and unease, which had been so much a feature of the evening, from disturbing their contemplation. Thoughts of the hateful intentions of Jerusalem's ungodly, Judas' betrayal and the horrors awaiting Jesus were kept at bay for that all-too-brief period. Instead, they were surrounded with the sublimity of the eternal realm which overshadows time, the place of unsurpassed beauty and splendour (John 17:5,22), enriched with joyful serenity (John 17:13).

There was also another dimension to the prayer. It concerned the 'little flock' for whom God's Son was soon to die. He would never have tantalized his sheep by opening the gate of heaven's fold ajar and allowing them a brief glimpse of its 'many mansions' (John 14:2) and the vastness of its expanse, unless he intended to impress upon them the reality of it. The promise had already been given: 'My sheep hear my voice, and I know them, and they follow me: and I give unto them eternal life; and they shall never perish, neither shall any man pluck them out of my hand' (John 10:27-28).

They were to share in the perfect unity experienced within the Godhead (John 17:22), to behold the glory of the risen and ascended Christ (John 17:24) and participate in the love which the Father eternally expresses for his Son. In a beautiful prayer, which Paul cited to the Corinthians (1 Cor. 2:9), Isaiah foretold the blessings awaiting the people of God, for 'Since the beginning of the world, men have not heard, nor perceived by the ear, neither hath the eye seen, O God, beside thee, what he hath prepared for him that waiteth for him' (Isa. 64:4).

God's choice of his people

But how are these marvellous privileges secured? The prayer's third and final aspect also reveals the answer, unfolding the mystery which has always inflamed the world's anger and baffled many in the Christian church in succeeding generations. It is through the immensity of God's grace. The apostles had been taught by Jesus that their discipleship had by no means been accidental, that they were chosen by him (John 6:70), a fact which he had reiterated at the supper (John 15:16). Indeed, this truth applies to everyone born of the Spirit; he is drawn irresistibly to Christ at the Father's behest (John 6:44,65) and without this essential work of grace it is impossible to be reconciled to God, or be raised to everlasting life by the Son.

Now, in the prayer a new facet of this truth came to light. They were the Father's love-gift to the Son, known by name within the kingdom of God before time was conceived. Then, when the Son was 'daily his delight, rejoicing always before him' (Prov. 8:30), the Father recognized these men as his own: 'Thine they were, and thou gavest them me' (John 17:6). They obviously assumed their call to discipleship was the Son of God's first knowledge of them, but in fact they were known to him 'before the foundation of the world'! (John 17:24). When he came to earth, guided by the drawing power of the Spirit, he sought them out. Hence, the shock Nathanael (Bartholomew) received when Jesus said to him, 'Before ... Philip called thee, when thou wast under the fig tree, I saw thee.' The new disciple immediately understood the significance of what Jesus had said and responded with awe: 'Rabbi, thou art the Son of God; thou art the King of Israel' (John 1:48-49).

But the teaching affects every individual in his flock, 'them also which shall believe on me through their word' (John 17:20). They too were known to the God of their salvation prior to the dawn of history, their names written with the red ink of the Saviour's blood in the Lamb's book of life (Rev. 20:15). They share in the divine favour extended to the elect, the sheep for whom Christ died (John 10:15), and this particular grace assures them of the high-priestly compassion (Heb. 4:15) reserved for the Father's purchased possession (1 Peter 2:9-10). Like the men in the upper room, they too are a precious people for whom the ascended Christ prays as he sits at the Father's right hand (Heb. 1:3). He prays not for the world but for those whom the Father gave him, for 'All mine are thine, and thine are mine; and I am glorified in them' (John 17:10). He expects them to prove faithful to God's Word (John 17:6), which is revealed truth (John 17:17) and therefore unchangeable (John 10:35), and to reflect the unity they share with the triune God (John 17:22).

These are the privileged few (Matt. 20:16), the benefactors of Jesus' last will and testament (Heb. 9:15-28), who are as assured of God's present keeping power (1 Peter 1:2-5) as they are of future glory in heaven (John 17:24). The 'prince of this world' (John 14:30), the devil whose children they once were (John 8:44), has been overthrown for ever (Col. 1:13-14). His influence is still felt and at times the sheep wander into his meadows, but such is the power of Christ's blood that it cleanses from *all* sin (1 John 1:7). The elect have been justified in the eyes of divine justice (Rom. 5:1), sanctified by the indwelling Spirit (1 Cor. 6:11,19-20) and have every right to expect glorification (Rom. 8:30).

The prayer closed, the supper over, Jesus led his friends from the room into the cool night air. Not far away was a peaceful garden, a quiet place for prayer among the trees.

3.
Anguish in the shadows

Jerusalem is 2,500 feet above sea level. Although the city swelters under a blazing sun by day it cools considerably at night. Thus when Jesus and his friends quietly made their way through the deserted streets they probably wrapped their robes around them more securely against the chill breeze. Nervous tension only served to increase the discomfort.

He led the way down the slope into the Kedron Valley, towards Gethsemane, which nestled at the foot of Olivet. The stillness over the entire area created its own tension, shadows danced under the moon and the mood was grave. It was one the eleven had not experienced before, an oppression they were incapable of understanding. Suddenly, he turned to them and said quietly, 'All ye shall be offended because of me this night' (Matt. 26:31). They were astonished, but he reminded them of the prophet's warning, that if the Shepherd was killed the sheep would be scattered (Zech. 13:7).

Even if the Lord had spoken without reference to the Scriptures it should have been sufficient to silence them, but as was his custom, he rested his case upon revealed truth which rebuked their consciences that much more. Jesus sugared the pill by reminding them of his glorious resurrection, but they took no notice. Peter, echoing the others' thoughts, blurted out that even if everyone else was offended by the Master, he certainly would prove faithful! (Matt. 26:32-33). It was well for Peter the shadows hid Jesus' expression. Pride is never attractive, but its ugliness was enhanced in the vicinity of Calvary.

To Peter's consternation, Jesus persisted. Not only would Peter be offended when the darkest of moments arrived, he would even publicly deny he knew Jesus. And he would do so three times! As if anticipating the obvious question, Jesus answered it for him. Despite his fine words and confident assurances, Peter would find himself in the doldrums within a few hours: in fact, at dawn, when cocks crow (Matt. 26:34). Crowing should be left to cockerels, not to men!

Like Jesus' hurt, Peter's embarrassment was mercifully hidden in the shadows. Only his voice could be heard feebly attempting to justify himself and bolster his flagging spirits. The others, though, were in no position to gloat. They knew Peter spoke for them too. He tried once more, insisting that he was more likely to die with Jesus than deny him (Matt. 26:35). The others also sought to impress the Lord. They too would never falter in their courage and devotion. The reality, within hours of their boasting, as Jesus knew, was going to be very different.

The garden of Gethsemane

The discussion over, they crossed the Kedron Valley and ascended the green slope which formed part of the Mount of Olives. There, silhouetted against the moonlit sky, they saw the familiar sight of a grove of gnarled olive trees, the garden of Gethsemane. Sensing danger, with Judas and his allies not far off, Jesus instructed eight of his friends to remain on guard at the entrance. The others, Peter, James and John, who were more akin to him at that stage in spiritual matters, he invited to accompany him further into the garden, where the trees were more abundant and the undergrowth luxuriant (Matt. 17:1; 26:36-37).

From this quiet spot, through the overhanging branches of the trees where a gentle breeze wafted, could be seen Jerusalem's walls, standing tall and firm. There too was the gate (the Golden Gate) through which a few days earlier Jesus had ridden in triumph amid the heat and clamour of the crowds (Matt. 21:1-17). By contrast, in the cool shades of the garden he discovered the necessary solitude required for reflection and prayer. It would not last long. Soon, Gethsemane's tranquillity would be shattered, the air filled with the aggressive coarseness of the ungodly looking for their prey.

The final battle with Satan approaches

Jesus was in no doubt what lay ahead of him. On more than one occasion he had warned the disciples about it. He was going to be arrested by the authorities and 'suffer many things' before being killed (Matt. 16:21). In Gethsemane, he waited for the inevitable and no doubt thought about the man leading the procession towards him at that moment. What hurt he had caused! The betrayal, although expected, was nevertheless a sharp thorn which penetrated Jesus' pure heart. The prophet painted the picture accurately when he described it as a 'wound' inflicted in the house of friends (Zech. 13:6). Who else but Jesus could still love such an enemy, and a child of hell? (Matt. 5:44). Even as Judas was in the act of betraying him to the authorities, Jesus could still call him 'friend' (Matt. 26:50). The fact that Judas had indeed been numbered among his friends increased the strain Jesus was under.

He understood more than anyone that his betrayer's entry into the drama was not an accident of history, but rather was an essential part of heaven's plan, in which the Scriptures would be fulfilled to the letter. He could not erase from his mind the anguish he had felt at the supper shortly before when, as God the Son, he had seen the horror of hell reserved for the devil and the fallen angels (Matt. 25:41), as he looked into the eyes of one destined for that place (Acts 1:16-25).

At this point, the reader may ask the obvious question: if God sovereignly ordained the dramatic events under review, including the raising up of the leading personalities involved in them, how was it possible for the Son of God to pity Judas? How can the betrayer be condemned by the Judge, when it was he who was responsible for putting him in the dock? Replying against God is always a dangerous occupation, but questions will inevitably be asked along these lines (Rom. 9:19-20).

The answer lies not in the relationship between Jesus and Judas, but in that between God and man. Even Christians, perhaps mercifully, do not appreciate the appalling consequences of man's fall in Eden (Gen. 3). The matchless perfection of God had come into contact with sin, and to be true to his nature, there was only one thing to expect. Not only was the entire creation cursed (Rom. 8:22), but in the persons of Adam and Eve God drove mankind from his presence, beyond Eden's gate, and set cherubim to guard it with a flaming sword. Had this not happened, God's integrity would have been compromised. Deity without honour is also without worshippers, or at least it should be.

The Fall was total. Man was not unconscious, but 'dead' (Gen. 2:17): dead in his soul and dead to any ability to please his Maker (Rom. 8:8). On the wrong side of Eden, having forfeited all the privileges and benefits of intimate fellowship with the divine (Gen. 3:24), man finds himself alienated, a stranger in a cold world, incapable of returning to God on his own terms — and, alarmingly, dead to any desire to do so (1 Cor. 15:22). That being so, he has no arena in which to debate with heaven — and no case to present. All he can do is hang his head in shame, and hold his tongue in silence. Whatever happens after that is the prerogative of the living God, whose activity among men is 'according to the good pleasure of his will' (Eph. 1:5).

It was not surprising, therefore, that Gethsemane witnessed such anguish that Thursday night. Satan's presence was almost tangible, for God in Christ had come to man's aid and the enemy of souls was cornered and at his most fierce (1 Peter 5:8). The greatest of all conflicts was about to begin. Heaven was taking the battle to the gates of Satan's kingdom. In a public display, the prince of death (John 14:30) would be overthrown by the Prince of life (Acts 3:15). Satan's back would at last be broken (Col. 2:15) and the devil's 'works' finally destroyed (1 John 3:8).

At the centre of the strife stood Jesus, in the most isolated position there could be, and the one that brought him into focus on the world's stage. Men may not appreciate the reasons for his appearance, or believe in him at all, but they should recognize a true

man when they see one in an age when Christianity is considered the
domain only of women and children. In a film some years ago, the
actor portraying Christ shaved the hair from his armpits! If even in
Christendom effeminacy is often mistaken for holiness, weakness
for meekness, it is vital to remember the essential masculinity of
Jesus of Nazareth. To follow him is to 'endure hardness' (2 Tim.
2:3).

Equally, it is important not to swing to the other extreme. He was
every inch a man, the Son of man, but (and I write reverently) not
Superman. The fictional character would not have confronted his
enemies (except to floor them!), but rather would have flown away
far and above them out of their reach. Jesus was not a romantic figure
stepping from a novel; he met the opposition head on, and his
sufferings were as real as his person and the 'strong crying and tears'
he shed in his extreme affliction (Heb. 5:7).

Jesus' vigil in the garden was a lonely one, despite the presence
of his friends, for upon his shoulders rested the unique responsibility
of opening heaven's mighty gates. Nobody else could do it; everything depended upon him (Rev. 1:18). Without his ministry — and
there could not be another opportunity — those gates would be
locked and barred for ever. The prospect was grim if he failed:
humanity doomed from the womb, with everlasting condemnation
in hell waiting at the end of life's road. However, should he succeed,
heaven's anthem of praise to the Lamb of God would be sung
everlastingly by myriads redeemed by his atoning sacrifice (Rev. 5;
7). The challenge was stark, the consequence everlasting: heaven or
hell, glorious success or abysmal failure — all or nothing.

Somewhere in the distance flickering flames could be seen, and
excited voices heard, as Jesus waited for the curtain to rise and the
drama to commence. Satanic oppression overwhelmed him and the
eleven with him, bringing with it exhaustion of mind and body. The
disciples were probably unaware of why they were so drained of
energy. They were strong, used to spending entire nights pulling in
the nets on Galilee's lake (Luke 5:5), but they had never felt so
weary before. Jesus understood.

Peter, James and John had not seen him like this before. He who
had walked the length of Israel, vigorously preaching and healing,

had put to flight the fury of the priests and audaciously swept out the temple on two occasions in a fearful display of righteous anger, was now 'exceeding sorrowful, even unto death' (Matt. 26:38). It was as if he had entered a dark room and was closing the door behind him, permitting no one to follow, sombre and subdued. Contemplative, for once aloof, he was about to walk across the deepest of valleys along the tightest of ropes.

He instructed the three to remain where they were, and to pray for deliverance from temptation. It seemed strange that a peaceful garden could prove a rendezvous with danger, but that night the atmosphere was such that anything could have happened. Within Gethsemane were two powers on the eve of the bloodiest battle known to man. God the Son had witnessed Satan's fall from heaven (Isa. 14:12-15) and man's fall from favour (Gen. 3). When an infant he had risked Satan's retaliation (Rev.12) and an attempted assassination (Matt. 2:16); and as an adult a second attempt on his life (Luke 4:28-29), as well as the tempter's subtle provocations (Matt. 4:1-11). Now Christ and Satan were confined to the same small garden, the former by man and the latter by God.

Jesus prays to his Father

Jesus made his way deeper into the grove of olive trees, a stone's throw from where Peter, James and John were seated (Luke 22:41). They watched him silently from under a bright moon, and knew he was not to be disturbed. His mind was not in Gethsemane but elsewhere, under the weight of an excessive burden, conscious of Skull Hill waiting in the darkness not far away.

When the cross claimed him it would be the culmination of a long expectancy, within heaven and also on earth as a result of centuries of gradually unfolding revelation. Prophets had foretold the event (1 Peter 1:9-12), sages sighed over it (Luke 2:29-30) and ordinary people yearned after it (Luke 1:41-42). Now at last, after generations of waiting, since the dawn of history in fact (Gen. 3:15), the moment was on the brink of fulfilment.

The awareness of his responsibility, and the acute isolation it had brought him, drove him to the only place where consolation could be found (2 Cor. 1:3-4). His three friends watched as Jesus collapsed on the ground and prayed. They could hear his voice: 'O my Father, if it be possible, let this cup pass from me: nevertheless not as I will, but as thou wilt' (Matt. 26:39). It was a cry of aching intensity. Listening to him speaking to the Father had always been a rare and remarkable experience, but that night was special. As someone said, a man is what he is when he is on his knees, and nowhere else.

What poignancy was expressed in a prayer beginning with the single-letter word, 'O'! It conveyed emotion rising to the surface from deep within (Isa. 64:1), which only the Father, the 'Lord of heaven and earth', could understand (Matt. 11:25). It reflected the unspoken language of the heart, the 'groanings which cannot be uttered' (Rom. 8:26) which are the prayers most welcomed at the throne of God (Ps. 51).

But when that seemingly inconsequential word 'O' was accompanied by another word of one syllable, 'my', and applied to the Source of all grace and strength, Jesus' heart required nothing else. It transported his spirit beyond time to when he was daily the Father's delight, 'rejoicing always before him' (Prov. 8:30). How he longed to return! Having experienced the mystery of oneness with the Father and the Holy Spirit, he, and only he, is permitted to say '*my* Father'. The nearest his disciples can get is in the acknowledgement that he is '*our* Father' (Matt. 6:9).

Jesus' prayer could have consisted of only three words, 'O, my Father', there being no need to say more. His intense anguish was adequately summed up in that phrase and the message received and understood in heaven. But for posterity's sake, audible references were made to his thoughts and feelings. He knew the extent of the sufferings he would have to endure, and he contemplated them with trepidation and loathing — a very human reaction. This is especially so when we consider that his destiny was to endure the torments of the damned in hell, intensified within the space of three hours (Matt. 27:45). He was not a romantic hero, a figment of the imagination with nerves of steel, but flesh and blood. The true heroism was to be seen in that, despite his horrendous fears, he was able to add, with utter devotion and total submission to the Father's plan and purpose, 'Not as I will, but as thou wilt' (Matt. 26:39).

As for Peter and the two brothers, their attempts at intercession were short-lived, as one by one weariness overcame them. On the eve of such a momentous occasion, with satanic powers within reach, the three who were closest to him slumbered! Their careless-ness defied the warning Jesus had given to Peter earlier in the evening of Satan's particular interest in him (Luke 22:31-32). The enemy of souls would prefer to watch a man sleeping than praying, a maxim Peter eventually learned to apply. Vigilance in the presence of the adversary is the best policy (1 Peter 5:8).

Peter awoke to find a disappointed Jesus standing beside them: 'What, could ye not watch with me one hour?' (Matt. 26:40). One prayerful hour on such a night was not asking much. As in every generation, the Lord needed to alert the indolent spirit among his disciples to the dangers surrounding them. He urged them to 'watch and pray', but the flesh proved much weaker than the spirit (Matt. 26:41). They slept again.

Jesus' period of prayer revealed how troubled he was (Matt. 26:39-44). He, who was used to praying throughout nights spent on tranquil mountains, was restless in Gethsemane, finding it difficult to remain in one place. Clearly he was no stoic who believed he could handle the situation without seeking help, but even though he was God he was also manifest in flesh. How honoured were his three companions that the Son of man, leaving the throne of grace for a short while, should desire fellowship with mere mortals! But when he arrived they were sleeping.

Each visit to his friends proved disappointing and was a short one. If only they had understood his need of them! He returned to the secluded spot and continued praying. We note how his reaching out to the Father shone with purity; he did not seek to conceal his innermost feelings, as we might have done, but expressed them with refreshing honesty. Imagine, no less a person than the Son of God himself admitting he did not want to go to Calvary! (Matt. 26:39). Nor did he stop to consider whether his prayers were 'correct', and acceptable to those who were listening. Instead he threw himself to the ground, as did Moses (Exod. 34:8) and Aaron (Num.14:5), concerned with groaning not grammar, depth rather than length.

There was, however, something unusual about Jesus' prayers that night in Gethsemane. They were not only extremely short, but repetitive. He approached the heavenly throne 'saying the same words' (Matt. 26:44), not vainly like the heathen he had warned about, whose 'prayer' beads and 'prayerful' chants have more to do with magicians than with the living God (Matt. 6:7). Rather, because tension had taken control of his tongue and his mind was numbed by the circumstances, words were inadequate to keep pace with the flow of his feelings.

The appearance of the angel

Peter, James and John suddenly awoke, instinctively aware that something had happened. Providence had probably alerted them, since Jewish law demanded the presence of two or three witnesses before a 'matter' could be established (Deut. 19:15). Glancing around, they noticed a rare brilliance shining through the trees in the area where Jesus was praying. An angel had appeared (Luke 22:43).

The three quietly approached. They were not inexperienced in the unusual and supernatural, having been not long before what Peter was later to call 'eyewitnesses of his majesty' (2 Peter 1:16). Jesus had taken them with him to a mountain so that they might witness his 'transfiguration', when an unusual radiance bathed him in glory. It was reminiscent of Moses' appearance after his meeting with God on Sinai (Exod. 34:29-35). Even the Lord's clothing was the dazzling brilliance of light. That was not all. They saw two men speaking to him who they learned were Moses and Elijah, the former representing the law and the latter the prophets (Matt. 17:1-9). Eternity and time had overlapped for a few precious moments.

In Gethsemane it happened again. Jesus continued praying, apparently unaware of the presence of the angel beside him, yet visibly strengthened by it (Luke 22:43). The angel was merely a spectator, an encourager, nothing more than that. Nor could he be, for in the loving relationship between the Father and the Son what need was there of a stimulus? As Jesus had earlier told his friends at the supper, 'Believe me that I am in the Father, and the Father in me' (John 14:11). The angel was a 'ministering spirit' to support, comfort and encourage the Son in his adversity, a reminder in that dark period of his Father's constant care and concern (Heb. 1:13-14).

Peter, James and John were quite close to the incident, no doubt standing silently in the shadows, for they observed certain details which otherwise would have gone unnoticed. For instance, they detected sweat on Jesus' forehead despite the cool night air, which made them realize how much strain he was under. What shocked them, however, was that mingling with the sweat was blood (Luke 22:44). Probably Doctor Luke, the 'beloved physician' (Col. 4:14), later provided the diagnosis. Hematidrosis is a rare condition resulting from extreme pressure, when the minute blood vessels beneath the skin burst. The 'bloody sweat' ran so freely down his face that the ground upon which he knelt was damp.

The angel left as suddenly as he had appeared, for angels never linger, and the three astonished spectators quietly returned to their resting-place too exhausted to talk about what they had seen. Instead, surrounded by peace disturbed only by the rustle of leaves above their heads, they closed their eyes and slept. How long they slept they did not know, but they were awoken by Jesus' gentle reminder that 'The hour is come; behold the Son of man is betrayed into the hands of sinners. Rise up, let us go.' The betrayer had arrived (Mark 14:41). They hurriedly jumped to their feet. This was it!

The arrest

Almost immediately, the garden's tranquil atmosphere was swept aside by aggressive activity. First through the olive groves, running swiftly towards them, came their fellow disciples. One suspects they had also been asleep, but the advancing crowds had woken them up and like sheep they had not known what to do. Their heads told them to run away, but their hearts dictated that they enter the garden to warn Jesus and their friends. By the time they reached them, it was too late to return the way they had come: the hunters would have met them head on.

They were all trapped, and could only wait for the pursuers to reach them. The noise of angry shouts and tramping feet grew louder, and shortly afterwards, accompanying it was the sight of numerous flames dancing towards them. Gethsemane, no longer a secluded garden, was swathed in artificial light, the glint of steel much in evidence. Judas led the way, having guessed Jesus would go to Gethsemane after the supper, eager to accomplish his task and fulfil his role. He was followed by high-ranking members of the Sanhedrin and officers and men of the temple guard (Luke 22:52). All this to arrest one man! (John 18:3).

They were well prepared; nothing was going to hinder an arrest. The authorities wondered whether even at that late hour, in more ways than one, the people would revolt in their support of Jesus. After all, he had been extremely popular only a few days before (Matt. 21:8-9). Therefore to prevent trouble, a force had been assembled to assure Jesus' safe passage to the high priest's residence with the minimum of fuss.

Aggression had driven them to the venue, but once there they appeared to be at a loss to know how to proceed, expecting resistance of some kind. Instead, Jesus stood quietly waiting for whatever was to occur. Subsequent events showed that the eleven were agitated,wondering what to do, but they were almost completely overlooked. It was Jesus whom the intruders were interested in.

Judas, with the audacity he had shown at the supper, approached Jesus as one greeting a friend. Treachery's kiss had been arranged as a signal of recognition (Mark 14:44), but the plan to have Jesus arrested did not immediately take effect. Somehow, despite the fact that he was defenceless, those nearest to Jesus seemed reluctant to rush forward to grab him as would have been their custom. There was a 'presence' about him which the temple guards could not fathom. This was no ordinary 'criminal'!

For three years Jesus had been the most controversial citizen in the country. His fame and influence stretched from one end of Israel to the other, including both sides of the River Jordan, and even throughout Syria (Matt. 4:24-25). His multitudes of followers had at one stage even sought to make him a king (John 6:15). They were constantly amazed by his miraculous powers, just as the authorities felt threatened by his presence. Only the previous Sunday Jesus had, for the second time, provoked the establishment and alarmed everyone within reach by driving the money-changers from the temple in an act of righteous vengeance against corruption (Matt. 21:12-13; cf. John 2:13-17).

So the guards' hesitation was understandable. It was left to Jesus to enquire whom they were seeking. He was obliged to ask twice, because after his acknowledgement that he was their prey, their reaction startled the onlookers. They 'went backward', falling to the ground (John 18:6). Satan's envoy was capable of looking his Master in the eyes, even in the act of betrayal, yet those who had not had the privilege of walking with him every day for years were unable to stand in his presence. They surely wondered why they acted as they did. There was 'something' about his open and steady gaze, the eyes being the mirror of the soul, that prevented them from doing so. Darkness must always give way to light.

Jesus had not moved. There was no heroic stance, no sudden demonstration of divine powers. Upon being told they were looking for Jesus of Nazareth, he had merely said, 'I am he' (John 18:5,8). That was all. He had looked his opponents in the eyes, and that was sufficient to humble them. The contrast between the hunters and the hunted could not have been more stark. Their rugged enmity was offset by his quiet and dignified calm, their guile by his pure gaze. It was never going to be straightforward trying to arrest the Son of God.

The atmosphere was electric, and dangerous. No longer was the garden the peaceful spot it had been a short time before. Now, there was the noise of jostling crowds, argumentative officials and impatient temple guards anxious to secure an arrest as quickly as possible. With Jesus were the agitated apostles, unsure of what to do, or what was likely to happen to them all. Between the two parties the atmosphere could have been cut with a knife. Only Jesus remained calm in the midst of them all.

Suddenly what had been threatening occurred. The tension snapped like a taut bowstring. Sadly, the initial move came from Jesus' party. Concealed within Peter's robe was a weapon, a short dagger or 'sword'. He had evidently understood Jesus' words literally, when in the upper room earlier that evening the Lord, speaking metaphorically, had warned the disciples of the future dangers they faced after he had left them. In underlining these perils, he had suggested, 'He that hath no sword, let him sell his garment, and buy one' (Luke 22:36).

With his usual impetuosity, Peter made sure he secured a sword as quickly as possible! The others had probably not realized he had a weapon, but once they saw it they gained a kind of 'Dutch courage'. What was one small sword against so many? Like the heroes they did not feel, they shouted to their Lord, 'Lord, shall we smite with the sword?' (Luke 22:49). Before Jesus had time to reply, and as hands reached out to grab him, Peter slashed out and the nearest person to him received the blow. It happened to be Malchus, the high priest's servant, whose ear was sliced off.

It had been a foolish and dangerous thing to do. With the highly trained guards nearby aching for action, men could have died that night, and Peter would have been the first. Jesus hurriedly stepped in, making no attempt to hide his displeasure, commanding his wayward apostle to sheathe his dagger, and adding sharply, 'The cup which my Father hath given me, shall I not drink it?' (John 18:11). Once again, as at the supper a few hours earlier (John 13:6-8), Peter had revealed his unwillingness to accept the ways of God (Matt. 16:21-23).

His problem was that, with misconceived bravery, Peter had felt obliged to back up his earlier boasting with practical action (Matt. 26:33,35). There was also another reason. With the others, he had been raised in the rabbinical teaching that the expected Messiah was to be a political figure with the overthrow of the Roman occupation of Israel his prime aim (Acts 1:6). The events in the garden appeared tailor-made for the realization of the plan.

Surrounded by his enemies, it was not the best time for Jesus to have to give Peter and the others lessons about the plan of salvation. They should have learned them already. In the heat of the moment, all Jesus could do was to elevate his poor students' thinking. After all the teaching, did Peter not appreciate that what was happening was the fulfilment of the Scriptures? Far from his being ineffective and at the mercy of the mob, Jesus was victoriously within the will of his Father. Did he not believe that there were 'twelve legions of angels' at his command had he wanted them to come to his aid? (Matt. 26:53-54). A Roman legion consisted of about 6,000 men, so that means 72,000 angels! (Heb. 1:4).

Despite their carnal way of thinking, the disciples were familiar with the teaching about heavenly beings, how that they surround the throne of God and worship him without ceasing (Isa. 6:1-3). Not only had the rabbis taught it to these men from childhood, but more especially the subject had featured in Jesus' lessons to them (Matt. 25:31). In any case, they had heard Mary speak of her experience of what had happened just over thirty years earlier when Gabriel visited her (Luke 1:26-27). She had also fascinated them with the accounts of the angelic visitations to John the Baptist's father (Luke 1:5-11), to the man to whom she was betrothed (Matt. 1:20) and also to certain shepherds in Bethlehem (Luke 2:8-14). In the light of all this, how strange it was that after their experience of seeing an angel Peter, James and John just went back to sleep! (Luke 22:43-45).

While everyone was momentarily silenced by Peter's violent behaviour, Jesus quickly responded by healing the victim and in doing so defused an inflammatory situation. His graciousness prevented a bloodbath, but it also had the effect of switching the spotlight from Peter back to himself, a situation he welcomed. This unselfish thinking was typical, his main concern being for his disciples, as his prayer in the upper room had intimated (John 17:12). He did not want them hurt, and sought their release from the predicament they were in (John 18:8-9).

Jesus reasoned with the intruders, speaking to their consciences. He questioned why their leaders felt it necessary to go to such lengths — the arrest of one person hardly justifying the use of a small army with an array of weaponry. In any case, why had they not arrested him in broad daylight and in the public arena of the temple, where they knew he could be found every day? (Matt. 21:23,45-46). The answer was known to everyone. Seeking their prey after dark when the city was asleep was wiser in the council's estimation.

The healing of Malchus proved beneficial not only to the man himself, but also to the eleven. After Peter's outburst they all feared the worst. The blade flashing in the torchlight had given the impression to the guards that they were all armed. Fearing an onslaught, they sought a way to escape, but the opportunity did not arise until after the miraculous healing. It caused such a stir that the curious onlookers scarcely noticed them slipping away in the shadows, and running in various directions through the trees — that is, until it was too late. How strange, though, that they forsook the security of the one who had 72,000 angels at his command!

By the time they were missed, although the guards searched the garden, the scattered flock, unhampered by heavy clothing, had sped away to comparative safety to await events (Zech. 13:7), their earlier boasting of undivided loyalty to their Master now decidedly hollow (Matt. 26:30-35).

They were followed by a young man whose narrow escape from arrest had cost him his clothing, though his youthful agility had served him well. The youth was more than likely John Mark, for why should the Gospel in his name be the only one to mention the incident? (Mark 14:51-52). Presumably, he had forsaken his bed upon hearing the tramp of many feet and the shouts of the crowd as it made its way towards Gethsemane. Dressing swiftly, and inadequately for the night air, he had left his home eager to witness the drama (Acts 12:12). It is not known at what stage he entered the garden, but his curiosity brought him within sight and sound of what he had come to see.

Jesus was now bereft of friends, alone with his captors, who savoured their moment of triumph, the arrest without difficulty of Jesus of Nazareth. It had taken three frustrating years for the Sanhedrin to achieve his apparent downfall. The stern and ruffian guards surrounding him, the self-satisfied and grinning priests, made sure they were not going to lose him now. It had been a good night's work.

Jerusalem slept, with dawn still a few hours away, but some might have heard the sound of rejoicing crossing the Kedron Valley towards the city gate from the direction of Gethsemane. Flaming torches swaying to and fro, the excited chatter of a jostling crowd, the rustling robes of the priests, the shuffling of sandals on the dusty road: these signified the beginning of Jesus' spiralling descent into the vortex of violence and accompanying agony.

4.
When cocks crow

Facing Jesus were two exhausting trials, one ecclesiastic and the other civil. Stage one of the first trial brought the prized captive to the house of Annas, the retired high priest, who had not held office for some years (since A.D. 14, when he had been deposed by the Roman procurator Valerius Gratus). However, despite retirement a high priest retained the title for the remainder of his life. It was, therefore, a matter of courtesy that the preliminary hearing was held in his presence (John 18:13,19-24).

The hearing before Annas

Jesus was led into the room where Annas sat waiting. The old man may not have seen Jesus before, but he had certainly heard of him. Indeed, with his son-in-law Caiaphas, he had been one of the prime movers behind his arrest. Not long before, the Sanhedrin, of which Annas was an honoured member, had met and planned Jesus' death (John 11:49-53). He was therefore interested in seeing him for himself, and hearing what he had to say.

Jesus knew what the outcome would be of the night's proceedings. Even as Annas cast his first glance at his victim, the plot dictated that the end result would be Jesus' execution. Anything Annas said would be merely academic, a mockery of justice, crass hypocrisy. As expected, Jesus was pressed to reveal the names, addresses and whereabouts of his followers (John 18:19). He did not reply, nor did he give a satisfactory answer when questioned about his teaching. He knew Annas was toying with him, like a cat with a mouse. As a leading member of the Sanhedrin, Annas already possessed an informed understanding of what Jesus had been preaching throughout the land, and where it differed from traditional beliefs (Mark 7:1-13). The council had discussed it often enough.

Jesus made no attempt to conceal his attitude towards Annas, who was a disgrace to his exalted office, a charlatan like his son-in-law. His silence revealed it. In better times the role of high priest, reserved only for those directly descended from Aaron's family (Exod. 28), had been a glorious calling from God unique in the annals of history. Woe betide those who contended for the position unlawfully! (Num. 17). But corruption set in during the inter-testamental period, and now confronting Jesus, the high-priestly ideal, was an appointee of unbelieving Sadducees, who in turn were vassals of Rome.

The questions remained unanswered. Instead, Jesus made it plain to all in the room that he was fully aware of the secrecy surrounding his arrest and trial. By contrast, he had preached 'openly to the world' in public arenas like the nation's synagogues and within the temple precincts. By saying, 'In *secret* have I said nothing' (John 18:20), Jesus exposed the backstairs intrigue which had created the situation in which he found himself.

Annas, on the other hand, sought to create the impression of being impartial by feigning ignorance of the facts. Jesus remained unimpressed, suggesting to him that he ought to discover for himself the answers to his questions by making enquiries from the ordinary people, for they knew what he had said (John 18:21). All in the room must have winced at that statement. They understood how much the priesthood envied Jesus' popularity with the man in the street (Matt. 27:18). At that, an officer of the temple guard approached the prisoner and struck him fiercely in the face (John 18:22). It was to be the first of many blows Jesus would receive that 'Good' Friday morning. The first session was over.

Peter's first denial

In the meantime, hidden away in the shadows on the road leading
from Gethsemane were two familiar faces. Once they realized the
temple guards had given up the chase, Peter and John returned to the
scene. They watched as Jesus was led away to Annas' palace and
followed from afar. When the crowd arrived and Jesus was taken
indoors, John knew of a way they could approach within hearing of
what was taking place inside. It was a brave decision, and a great
risk, for no doubt their faces were imprinted upon the memories of
those who had been chasing them not long before.

John's Galilean family, like many others, was in the fishing trade
(Matt. 4:21,22), and the fish caught in Galilee's famous lake was
sold throughout the land. At regular intervals John travelled to
Jerusalem selling fish, and Annas was one of his customers. That is
how an ordinary working man from the north 'was known unto the
high priest' in the south (John 18:15). John had often appeared at the
gate of the courtyard with his basket of fish and spoken to Annas'
servant. On the night in question she proved useful to John, if
embarrassing to Peter.

The maid, seeing John, allowed him entrance into the courtyard,
through which he passed on his way to the main appartments of the
palace overlooking it. No doubt, John carefully looked around for
a spot where he and his friend could hear the proceedings against
Jesus, yet remain hidden from view. When his aim had been
achieved he returned to the gate outside of which Peter had been
nervously waiting. Not long before he had cut off the ear of the high
priest's servant!

At this point John made a foolish error. Perhaps he was urged on
by his eager friend, who was still seeking to honour his earlier
boasting to Jesus. Peter had not been very successful thus far, merely
proving an embarrassment, a clumsy attempt at heroism in
Gethsemane having been followed by a hasty and ignominious exit
from the scene. Now, he may have insisted to John that he must get
within close range of Jesus, so that he might be *seen* to be loyal. John
unwisely fell in with his suggestion. At the gate, he asked the maid
whether his friend might be allowed to enter. She agreed, and Peter

stepped out of the shadows for the first time since he left the upper room, into the halflight created by the flames of a nearby fire. Without thinking, John turned on his heels and disappeared into the main building, perhaps assuming Peter was following close behind.

In fact he lingered, and once inside the courtyard realized how conspicuous he was. Of all the disciples in the garden, Judas excepted, he had made the most lasting impression on the minds of the Sanhedrin officials and officers of the temple guard. He had been the man with the dagger offering a token resistance. Although in shadow, his face might have been remembered, a risk Peter now found himself having to take. He was in a quandary. Should he follow John or remain where he was? The awkwardness of such a situation invariably encourages bystanders to stare.

The woman at the gate was the first to detect that something was wrong. She gazed at Peter intently before enquiring of him whether he was a disciple of Jesus (Luke 22:56). Under normal circumstances the woman's inquisitiveness would not have presented any problems. If the need had arisen the strong fisherman could easily have brushed past her and made his exit. However, they were not alone. Huddled around the fire were some men, no doubt discussing the dramatic events of the night. They were probably temple guards, or palace servants. The guards out at that time, just before dawn, would have been among those who had chased Peter. Now, here he was, standing a few feet away! The maid's question was of more than academic interest for them.

Peter felt that his only recourse was to blurt out his reply quickly to cover his guilt. 'I am not,' he stated sharply (John 18:17). He had to be quick-thinking. On the one hand, he could not afford to remain with the suspicious woman, but on the other, seeking to escape the men would have caused them to give chase. There was only one avenue left to him, risky though it was. He had to join the men by the fire, possibly his recent hunters, as if he were associated with Jesus' enemies. In other words, far from demonstrating his loyalty, Peter was getting more entangled and further removed from his boasting promises (Matt. 26:33-35). Whatever else happened, he knew he was trapped in the courtyard. Leaving it at that moment would have created even greater suspicion (John 18:18).

The trial before Caiaphas

Living in another part of the palace was Joseph Caiaphas, the presiding high priest, to whom Jesus was now sent. This meant that he and his captors walked along the extended balcony which overlooked the courtyard below (Mark 14:66). Peter and his companions, warming themselves by the fire, must have caught a glimpse of him. Peter's feelings at that time are not recorded, but one can imagine what they must have been.

Caiaphas was waiting for the prisoner, and with him were the members of the council. The matter confronting them all was believed to be urgent enough to bring them from their beds (Matt. 26:57). In a sitting convened some time earlier, they had agreed at Caiaphas' suggestion that it was imperative to arrest and execute Jesus (John 11:49-53). This decision had later been confirmed (Matt. 26:3-4). The problem was that it required the official stamp of approval to satisfy all Jews, especially those multitudes which had followed him.

In any case, without the judgement receiving official sanction the Roman governor Pontius Pilate was not going to agree to it. So, despite the unusual hour, the members of the council were in bouyant mood. After years of seeking to destroy Jesus, at last they believed the process had begun. They could now go through the motions of holding a public hearing, even though the conclusions had already been agreed upon.

All eyes were upon Jesus as he entered the apartment set aside for the proceedings, including those of Peter, who had gained entrance by mingling with the servants (Matt. 26:58). Nobody was in any doubt about the illegality of what was about to take place, least of all the one who claimed that 'all judgement' had been committed to him by the Father (John 5:22). From the learned priests to the hastily cajoled witnesses willing to lie for a fee, all realized that what they were involved in was a travesty of justice. In fact it was to be the most notorious 'trial' in history.

As mentioned in the previous chapter, according to Jewish law, before an execution could take place two or three witnesses had to be produced in evidence against the accused (Num. 35:30). Prior to the gathering before Caiaphas there had been a hurrying and scurrying to and fro seeking the required number. The priesthood being very unpopular with the people, no one was prepared to assist them, even had they anything detrimental to say against Jesus. Caiaphas was reduced to seeking help from the lowest in society, from anyone who could be suborned to testify against him.

Jesus watched as one by one the witnesses appeared like clock-work to echo the accusations of their masters. The desire to destroy him was so great that the priests had scrambled with indecent haste to obtain their help. The rush appears to indicate the amount of activity there had been once Judas had informed the council where Jesus could be located. The result was that rehearsal time for what the witnesses would say in the court had been reduced to a mini-mum. So although there were many witnesses, far more than were required, they contradicted each other! (Mark 14:56). Caiaphas and his fellow conspirators blushed as the witnesses repeatedly gave the game away.

Jesus was not amused by the farce unfolding before him. He did not say anything, but simply gazed at Caiaphas and his false accusers. There had been a flagrant breach of the moral law. Written on the second tablet of stone by almighty God himself (Exod. 32:16), and given to Moses to pronounce to the people, were the words of the ninth commandment: 'Thou shalt not bear false witness against thy neighbour' (Exod. 20:16). Yet in the courtroom there were those who saw nothing wrong in breaking God's law, and did so for shekels. Much worse, the priests, whose task it was to uphold and teach the law, actually encouraged the breaking of it, in an endeavour to destroy its Author.

Eventually, two came forward and opened up an area of accu-sation. They both observed that Jesus had said, 'I am able to destroy the temple of God, and to build it in three days' (Matt. 26:61). These words were like music to Caiaphas' ears, and to those of his fellow priests. At last they had something they could use against the accused. The temple in Jerusalem involved everyone in the land: the priests, the people as a whole and even the Romans. The fact that the quotation was a jumbled half-truth spoken three years earlier was immaterial to Caiaphas and the court. The half-truth is as much a weapon of Satan's as the downright lie, and can create more mischief.

What Jesus had actually said at the time following the first cleansing of the temple was: 'Destroy this temple, and in three days I will raise it up' (John 2:19). He did not say he would destroy it, or that he could rebuild it at all, and certainly not in three days. His spiritual lesson relating to his resurrection on the third day was lost on the ungodly. They had no knowledge of what was due to take place on the Day of Pentecost, when God the Holy Spirit would descend with mighty power (Acts 2). Since that momentous occasion each individual indwelt by him is a temple far more precious to heaven than any manufactured temple (1 Cor. 3:16; 6:19-20). His critics could not be expected to grasp that sublime truth either.

Instead, they latched upon the word 'temple'. Jesus of Nazareth had said he was able to destroy the temple in Jerusalem, and rebuild it in a mere three days! It had taken forty-six years to build, and was still to be completed (John 2:20). In fact, they were to keep adding to its splendour for another thirty years. 150 feet in height, it was famous for its architectural grandeur, its huge colonnades and ornate carvings, and was considered by all who saw it as one of the wonders of the world. The rabbis suggested that anyone who had not seen it had not seen an impressive building in his life. The idea that anyone should wish to destroy so magnificent an edifice was unthinkable, even if he intended rebuilding it. It was the house of God, and the pivot around which Israelite life revolved.

Caiaphas knew he had Jesus where he wanted him. The people, with whom Jesus was so popular, would never understand such a sacrilegious intention and would surely turn from him in disgust. The same was true of the priests — if they needed any encouragement. As for the Romans, the temple had been built in honour of Cæsar. Herod the Great had ordered its construction in 20 B.C. to replace Solomon's temple, restored after the Exile 500 years earlier (Ezra 6). To destroy the temple, or even to think of doing so, was an affront to the emperor.

Sensing triumph, Caiaphas rose to his feet and challenged his prisoner to reply to the charge. Jesus refused to answer. He knew the two men were dupes in the hands of experienced knaves. They were merely mouthing the words of Annas and Caiaphas. These cunning culprits, being Sadducees, had a particular interest in the temple, the Romans having entrusted the Sadducean party with its custodianship. Jesus remained silent, the 'sheep' who, as Isaiah prophesied, 'opened not his mouth' (Isa. 53:7).

His calm dignity infuriated Caiaphas. It was clear that Jesus intended remaining silent throughout the hearing. Peter, who was watching the scene, was so deeply moved by his Lord's demeanour that he mentioned it many years later when writing to persecuted Christians. He recorded that there was no 'guile found in his mouth', that 'When he suffered, he threatened not, but committed himself to him that judgeth righteously' (1 Peter 2:22-23).

Caiaphas waited, but there was no response from Jesus. Something had to be done to force the remarkably patient prisoner to speak. Perhaps the emphasis ought to be changed, from his supposed statements about the temple to his claims about himself.

Caiaphas, no longer presiding as a chairman of an official hearing but as a self-appointed judge, feared Jesus' silence would cause the proceedings to grind to a halt. He therefore, craftily, decided to speed them up by changing the line of enquiry. To do this he delved into ancient Jewish law, in which the hearing of a solemn oath ('swearing') demanded a truthful and immediate reply because it was made in the sight of God. Failure on the accused's part to obey was a serious offence (Lev. 5:1).

Caiaphas turned to Jesus and pronounced the oath: 'I adjure thee by the living God, that thou tell us whether thou be the Christ, the Son of God' (Matt. 26:63). The solemn words reverberated around the room causing everyone to react sharply. They had probably not expected this dramatic turn of events, although throughout his ministry in Israel the priests had longed for a moment like this (Matt. 21:23). How would Jesus react? What answer would he give?

His obedience to the law was absolute, for his function was to fulfil the law, not to destroy it (Matt. 5:17), and his response was immediate. However, not even Caiaphas expected the direct reply he received. Jesus simply said, 'I am.' The air was immediately filled with excited anticipation, consternation written across every face as the members of the Sanhedrin burst into agitated discussion with each other. Above the chatter, Jesus continued to shock them all: 'And ye shall see the Son of man sitting on the right hand of power, and coming in the clouds of heaven' (Mark 14:61-63).

Astonished incredulity rippled through the room. Caiaphas reacted passionately, clutching his clothing fiercely like a grief-stricken mourner (Matt. 26:65). Nothing so 'blasphemous' had been heard before: Jesus, the carpenter from Nazareth, standing before the court claiming to be the apocalyptic figure in Daniel's glorious vision! This 'Son of man' is pictured arriving 'with the clouds of heaven' and approaching the 'Ancient of days' as an equal. An exquisite passage reveals the majesty of the King of all kings, whose kingdom is everlasting, the Master whom all humanity serves (Dan. 7:13-14).

The apostle Paul had this portion of God's Word in mind when he referred to almighty God having 'highly exalted' Christ Jesus. He who was 'equal with God' condescended to enter this world in flesh, became obedient to the Father, suffered, bled and died upon the cross for sinners. No greater name is there than that of Jesus, and every being in heaven and upon earth should bow at its very mention and openly confess Christ's lordship, to the glory of God the Father (Phil. 2:6-11).

Many years later, as an old man, John, who was present in the room when Jesus' astonishing declaration was first heard, was visited by his risen and ascended Lord (Rev. 1:10-20). What he saw caused him to collapse before the Lord, who in turn compassion-ately assisted him to his feet. John noted the type of clothing worn by the King as Son of man, not unlike what he wore every day during his time here in the flesh, but the golden girdle had replaced his belt of cord or leather. Thus he who 'took on him the seed of Abraham', who was 'made like unto his brethren' and who 'was in all points tempted as we are, yet without sin', has ascended into heaven, having brought 'many sons unto glory' through his atoning sacri-fice, resurrection and ascension (Heb. 2:16,17; 4:15; 2:10). In other words, standing before John, as he had been standing before the astonished court, was the prophet Zechariah's eternal King-Priest (Zech. 6:12-13).

Unlike the Pharisees, the Sadducees did not recognize Daniel as a prophet, their Bible being the Pentateuch alone. Nor did they believe in a Messianic hope, or countenance a belief in an afterlife (Acts 23:8). However, that did not prevent them from reacting violently against Jesus in what passed for a courtroom. If the Pharisees despised his apparently 'blasphemous' ways, the Sadducees like Caiaphas were riled by his commanding presence.

It was a turning-point. Both parties heard Jesus clearly admit to being the Messiah, the Lord of glory. An opportunity had arisen for them to believe him, repent and own his deity. Instead, amidst the noise of general uproar was exposed the hardness of their hearts. Caiaphas relished his apparent victory, although his jubilation was hidden behind a façade of mock indignation. Above the tumult, he charged Jesus with blasphemy and called for an immediate decision by those present.

Of course, they realized that as a Sadducee Caiaphas was not a spiritually minded man and the word 'blasphemy' did not have any relevance for him, but everyone responded as he had hoped. 'Blasphemy' was an emotive term, but it served his purpose well at the time. He knew that any moderate Pharisees present would be less tolerant towards Jesus if charged with that crime. Thus they insisted that their prisoner was 'guilty of death' (Matt. 26:66). It was a foregone conclusion.

At that, the room erupted as pandemonium broke out. The pent-up enmity of the last three years was unleashed, the brittle dignity of the priests shattered, as they jumped up from their seats and swarmed around him in a demonstration of blind hatred. In no time, Jesus was hidden from Peter's view as he suffered a plethora of blows. They taunted him to his face, covered in their spittle. One can imagine what today's media would make of an Old Bailey trial in which the judge, members of the jury and all in the court viciously attacked the prisoner in the dock!

Peter denies Jesus again

Peter watched for as long as he could, or dared. As a muscular fisherman he might have been tempted to join the affray in support of his Master. The situation was beyond him, and he felt so inadequate. Failing to know what to do, he quickly left the room as the scuffling continued. Finding a quiet spot, if one was available, Peter stood pondering what he had witnessed and wondering what his next move ought to be. He must have missed John. Where was he? On the one hand he felt it wise to run from the palace, but on the other he was reluctant to leave the vicinity where Jesus appeared to be at the mercy of ungodly men.

He did not have sufficient time to arrive at any conclusion. Soon, he was joined by a woman who to his intense embarrassment loudly accused him of having been with Jesus 'of Galilee'. Those standing nearby heard her and began asking their own questions. The more Peter denied his knowledge of Jesus, the more his Galilean accent betrayed him. He quickly left them, but had not gone many paces when once more he was confronted by another palace maid. The situation was gaining momentum, increasingly alarming for Peter. She turned to the passers by that they might take note of her accusation (Matt. 26:69-71). He walked as quickly as he could from the palace porch into the courtyard, hoping to shake them off, but they followed him. The situation appeared hopeless.

By this time panic was taking control, the number following him increasing, as were the questions and accusations. Peter was at his wits' end, not knowing what to do. He could stand the pressure no more. Once more he denied that he knew Jesus, and then out of desperation did something which upon reflection would have shaken him to the core. Turning to those harassing him, he made a solemn oath, probably in the name of almighty God (Matt. 5:33-37).

It made no difference. As he tried to shrug them off and make his way nearer to the main gate, others joined the group. They were persistent. He just had to be a disciple of Jesus for it was evident by his accent that, like the prisoner, he too was a northerner. Peter reacted with increasing violence, shouting curses and fresh oaths. It was as if he wished to prove how far removed he was from the pure carpenter from Galilee (Matt. 26:72-74).

At that moment, one of the apartment doors on the balcony above the courtyard opened and Jesus, bruised and bleeding, was pushed through it unceremoniously by his guards. The priests had finished with him for the time being. The noise of their sudden appearance caused Peter and those surrounding him to glance upwards. Before Jesus was swiftly hustled away to a nearby cell, his eyes met Peter's in the halflight of a rising sun. In the distance a cock heralded the arrival of the dawn (Luke 22:60-61).

The expression on Peter's face as he recalled Jesus' prediction of a few hours earlier caused his oppressors to lapse into silence, as people tend to do in the presence of a man weeping uncontrollably. All pride broken, he hurried through the gate and along the road seeking a place of shelter, an opportunity to reflect upon the failures of the night. While he hid away in relative comfort, his Lord was imprisoned in a dank cell to await forthcoming events. Peter had tried hard to keep as close as possible to Jesus, but the circumstances had proved more than a match for him.

The Sanhedrin gives its verdict

As the Jews were not permitted to carry out executions but were obliged to depend upon the Romans, the members of the council were in a hurry (John 18:31). Before the people had awoken to a new day, the priests wanted their official verdict to be in the hands of the governor. Jesus was therefore brought back to face those who shortly before had wreaked vengeance upon him so unjustly (Luke 22:66). The antagonism had not abated; if anything it had worsened, the members of the council having suffered a sleepless night on his account.

The proceedings were brief, in fact 'rubber-stamped'. The Sanhedrin desired Jesus to implicate himself as quickly as possible, so that there would be no further delay before it condemned him and finished with the entire business. Caiaphas repeated the question which had caused such a stir at the hearing. Did he still claim to be the Messiah? Jesus, bearing the same dignified calm as before, answered by exposing the court's injustice. What was the purpose of his answering the question, since the court had already agreed upon the verdict? Even if he exercised the right of a condemned man and asked his judges certain questions, they would not have replied (Luke 22:67-68).

Without waiting for the council members to retaliate, Jesus reiterated his former statement, namely that he was the Messiah, and then declared, 'Hereafter shall the Son of man sit on the right hand of the power of God' (Luke 22:69). The statement, spoken as it was in such an arena, is the most astonishing in history. No one, least of all the learned priests to whom it was first spoken, can be left in any doubt as to its meaning: Jesus was God incarnate.

It was the biggest gamble man has ever taken: the moment when the Jewish council had to decide what to do with Jesus of Nazareth, and whether to believe his claims or not. Humanity has diced with its soul for the past two thousand years over the same issue, the most far-reaching decision an individual can ever make. Was this extra-ordinary carpenter from the poorest regions of Israel to be taken seriously, or should he be discounted? There can be no half-measures; the answer is 'Yes' or 'No', and there are no grey areas.

Was Jesus a charlatan, now dead and buried, or is he the Creator, Upholder and Heir of all things? (Heb. 1:2). Did not the power of his miracles (Mark 4:41), the wisdom of his teaching (Matt. 7:28-29), the purity of his living (John 8:46) and the graciousness of his dying (Luke 23:34) cry aloud that he was the expected Son of man? (Dan. 7:13-14). A balanced scriptural assessment of this fascinating person reveals why generations of those who have known him have willingly submitted everything to him. Countless numbers have died for him, and numerous others are prepared to do so even today. Across the centuries a hymn-writer ably expresses the Christian mood:

> This is my Friend,
> In whose sweet praise
> I all my days
> Could gladly spend.

To that simple testimony every follower of 'the man Christ Jesus' (1 Tim. 2:5) since he stood in Caiaphas' court will say, 'Amen'.

The reason is not difficult to find. Observing the evidence, they have believed his claims and entrusted their souls to his eternal care and safe-keeping. They are wise. Appearing before the throne of judgement, as all men must in their turn (2 Cor. 5:10), including those who sat in judgement at the 'trial' of God's own Son, how disastrous will be the outlook for unbelievers when they see who is seated in everlasting glory at the right hand of ultimate power (Luke 22:69).

The Sanhedrin, at this stage hushed by the awesome implication of Jesus' statement, was prepared only to ask him an official question: 'Art thou then the Son of God?' Jesus was not willing to bandy words, merely declaring that his accusers had said so. He had already expressed himself clearly, and the statement was not contested any further; their prisoner had said it all. The priests sat back, their work brought to a successful conclusion. It was probably Caiaphas who expressed the thoughts of everyone present that they did not require any more witnesses (Luke 22:66-71).

The prisoner was bound, and he made no attempt to struggle, knowing that this was his 'hour' (John 17:1). Caiaphas and his colleagues could not have anticipated the benefits which would flow from Calvary and the empty tomb. Nor could they have imagined the glory that lay ahead for myriads to come (Heb. 2:9-15). As for Jesus, he looked above and beyond the manacles and the distress of the immediate future, to the joy of the plan fulfilled (Ps. 16:11), the warmth of the Father's smile and welcome (Heb. 12:2), universal adoration and everlasting praise arising from the redeemed (Rev. 5; 7).

The guards led Jesus from the room, accompanied by the entire council, consisting of about seventy-two men (Num. 11:25-27). It had been a long night, but there was still no opportunity to rest. In fact, the proceedings were only half over. The Jewish church had delivered its judgement, now it was the turn of the Gentile state. If the former was notoriously unjust, the latter was infamously cruel. Jesus was bruised and extremely tired, but as he was led out towards the Roman governor's place of residence he knew worse was to follow — much worse (Luke 23:1).

5.
The Lamb, the eagle and the fox

The Roman procurator usually resided at Cæsarea, seventy miles north-west of Jerusalem, but on the occasions when the Jews held their feasts he lived in the city at the magnificent palace which had once belonged to Herod the Great. Nearby, and close to the temple, was the fortress of Antonia, the garrison of the Roman legionaries stationed in Jerusalem and the seat of government during his time in the city.

His move to Jerusalem, several times annually, was due to the influx of worshippers, most of whom had swarmed in from all over the land and from as far away as Egypt or even Europe (Deut. 16:16). The feasts stirred in Judaism the latent frustrations of a nation ruled over by a foreign power. Tensions ran high and trouble was never far away. As a result there was a need for the governor to be near at hand to hold the city with a tight rein, which Pontius Pilate did both contemptuously and cruelly.

The sun was rising over a waking city as Jesus arrived within sight of the fortress accompanied by his captors, his appearance like that of any prisoner of the period with his hands tied and led by a rope around his neck. It had not taken them long to reach Antonia for Caiaphas' palace was nearby. In front of the grand building, with its marble colonnades and wide, steep steps, was an impressive flat pavement 3,000 square yards in size and adorned with porticoes, fountains and colourful mosaics. Looking out across the wide expanse, Pilate had a beautiful panoramic view of Jerusalem, for the fortress had been built on part of the Temple Hill.

Once the main doors had been reached those who were with Jesus would go no further, this being Gentile territory (Eph. 2:11-12). To proceed further would have rendered these 'sons of the law' ceremonially unclean in their own eyes, for they had been so occupied during the previous twelve hours that they had not had time to prepare the passover (John 18:28). Their hypocrisy was such, they could not see that they feared ceremonial uncleanness more than moral impurity, as Jesus had earlier pointed out (Matt. 23:27), and their fastidious observance of the law's minutiæ had not prevented them from abusing and condemning innocence in a corrupt court. In any case, no self-respecting Jew dared have contact with the hated heathen. Even the early church had difficulty overcoming this tradition, and Peter was obliged to give account of his actions when he was commanded by the Lord to enter Cornelius' house (Acts 10:32-34; 11:1-3).

The delegation comes before Pilate

Pilate may have seen the party approaching because, despite the early hour, he was waiting for it, the meeting having been hurriedly arranged during the previous night's activities. In any case, he always expected trouble once he was in the city. As his visitors were announced he must have expressed his usual impatience that he was obliged to meet the Jewish delegation at the main door. It did not help him to appreciate the Jews or their religion any better.

When Pilate saw the entire Sanhedrin assembled in front of him, led by Caiaphas, he feared the worst, knowing that this was not an ordinary case he was being called upon to assess. As he glanced at Jesus standing silently in the midst of his accusers he took stock of the person he had heard so much about, the individual who had been the main topic of conversation in Israel for several years. So this was Jesus of Nazareth!

Pilate duly enquired after the official accusation, as would have been his custom on such occasions. He was cynical about the priests' motives for dragging their prisoner to him so early in the day, and they knew it: 'If he were not a malefactor, we would not have delivered him up unto thee' (John 18:30). The governor was answerable to the emperor in Rome for keeping the peace in a troublesome corner of the empire, and the Sanhedrin made it as difficult as possible for him to do so. As it was, Pilate's mishandling of the Jews had not gone unnoticed in Rome, and the Sanhedrin had only to register an official series of complaints and Pilate's governorship, if not his life, would have been sacrificed. Pilate knew he had to tread carefully.

Despite this, his impatience could not be restrained (John 18:31). If these meddling priests had condemned a fellow Jew, what was it to him? He had not realized the death penalty was involved, for the Jews were forbidden to execute an offender. All such cases had to be referred to the governor, that the Roman authorities might carry out the sentence. The Jews objected to the Roman interference in their affairs, but there was little they could do about the matter. Roman law had to be obeyed strictly .

The Jewish and Roman methods of execution differed. The Jews used stoning or strangling; the Romans crucified their victims. Jesus had made it plain he would be 'lifted up' (John 3:14), knowing the divine plan dictated the method to be employed for the sacrificing of the Lamb of God (John 12:32). He was appointed to be made a curse for sinners (Gal. 3:10,13), fulfilling the scripture that he who hangs upon a tree is 'accursed of God' (Deut. 21:23). When Jesus therefore was handed over to the Roman governor, the Jewish church and Roman state were satisfied that events were entirely in their hands, while in fact they were themselves tools in the hands of Providence (Acts 2:23).

Pilate wondered what crimes the prisoner had committed that warranted execution. The priests had discarded the charge of blasphemy for they knew it would mean nothing to a Roman. Instead they charged Jesus with 'perverting the nation' (Luke 23:1-2), but to sustain Pilate's interest in the case, they added that their prisoner had rebelled against Rome. He had refused to pay taxes to Cæsar and, worse, taught that he was the Messiah-King. Immediately, Pilate was on his guard for no more serious a charge could he imagine.

The Sanhedrin was lying, and Pilate probably guessed it, but he could not afford to take any chances. It was true that some of these men had challenged Jesus not long before about whether he was prepared to pay his taxes to Cæsar, but he had given the classic reply: 'Render therefore unto Cæsar the things which be Cæsar's, and unto God the things which be God's' (Luke 20:19-26). As for his claim to be a king rivalling the emperor, Jesus had refused to allow the people to make him one (John 6:15).

Pilate is out of his depth

Pilate called Jesus to him and together they went inside the main building. No doubt the priests were reluctant to let their prisoner out of their sight for fear of what he might say. However, whatever else can be said about Pilate, he was not foolish enough to believe all the Sanhedrin's accusations. He had no respect for its members, knowing they were envious of Jesus' reputation and following (Matt. 27:18).

Once inside the hall, Pilate and Jesus looked at each other closely. The governor was a typical Roman, hard and disdainful of the conquered races, cruelty and arrogance being his stock in trade. His reputation since becoming procurator in A. D. 26 was notorious. Two incidents had provided him with it. The first occurred shortly after taking office. Riding roughshod over Jewish susceptibilities, Pilate ordered his troops to bring the Roman insignia from Cæsarea to Jerusalem. Realizing the Jews would consider such an action sacrilegious, the troops travelled overnight. By the time the citizens had awoken, the symbols of conquest were to be seen in prominent places. This contemptuous act incited an uproar among the Jews, who for five days and nights laid seige to Pilate's residence in Cæsarea, risking their lives in the process. The new governor had tasted Jewish resilience the hard way.

On another occasion, when Jerusalem was suffering from a water shortage, Pilate built an aqueduct (the ruins of which can be seen to this day) which would stretch from the Pool of Siloam to the city centre. This might have appeared a sound idea, except for the fact that he raided the 'Corban', or sacred treasury, to pay for the enterprise, money supposedly dedicated to the Jewish God. Again, the Jews expressed their fury in Jerusalem's streets as protesters reacted violently against the insult to almighty God. Pilate retaliated by sending some soldiers disguised as Jews into the mob, with weapons hidden in their clothing. At the pre-arranged signal carnage followed, and many were trampled to death trying to escape. These and other similar conflicts encouraged the Jews' hatred of Pilate and all things Roman.

Yet there was 'something' about Jesus, the Jew from Galilee standing before him, that Pilate could not fathom, and it disturbed him. During the three sessions of interrogation he, the governor with Roman law and military might behind him, appeared agitated, as if seeking answers to deep-rooted questions: 'Art thou the King of the Jews?'; 'What hast thou done?'; 'Art thou a king then?'; 'What is truth?' (John 18:33,35,37,38); 'Whence art thou?' and 'Speakest thou not unto me?' (John 19:9,10).

By comparison, his strange prisoner was extraordinarily calm, mysterious and in the end noncommittal (John 19:9). The rôles of governor and prisoner appeared reversed. Pilate found himself slowly being drawn into a situation for which he was unsuited temperamentally and religiously; nor could he escape from it without a loss of prestige as a Roman official. He had not been in this position before.

The priests stir up the crowds

As the interrogation continued, the sun was rising in a clear spring sky and the city awaking to a rumour that Jesus, the prophet of Nazareth, had been arrested during the night and was incarcerated at the Castle of Antonia. Soon Jerusalem was filled with enquirers, the indignant and the curious, converging upon the governor's residence and waiting to see whether the rumours were correct. The air was filled with excitement as the people approached from all directions.

To begin with they had been sympathetic to Jesus. Only the previous Sunday they had waved palms and chanted their praises as he rode into Jerusalem (Matt. 21:8-9). Nothing had happened since then to make them change their minds, yet before lunchtime on that Friday morning the same excited crowds would be transformed into a seething mob of hatred demanding Jesus' crucifixion (Matt. 27:22-23). There must have been a sound reason for such an astonishing turnabout.

The answer lay not far away from where the crowds were standing. Several dozen high-ranking priests were grouped together discussing what might be happening within the hall behind the main doors which had been closed to them. The entire membership of the Sanhedrin was scarcely ever seen together in public; the situation therefore had to be at crisis level for this to occur. What the multitude did not know was that arrangements had already been made by this august body of priests and elders to change the general thinking of the people gathering in large numbers behind them. As many priests as could be mustered were to make their presence felt in the crowds on the pavement (Matt. 27:20).

At that time there were about 6,000 Pharisees in the land, apart from the Sadducees and scribes, and most of these were congregated in the Jerusalem-Jericho regions. It would have been a simple matter for the Sanhedrin to imprint its authoritative weight upon the priesthood, which in turn would persuade the people where their sympathies were supposed to lie. After all, the priests possessed the power of excommunication from the synagogue and could threaten any dissenters with its use if necessary (John 9:34).

A king without a visible kingdom

Pilate looked at the prisoner standing before him and sneered. Jesus was tired and dishevelled, a rope fastened his hands and hung from his neck. 'Art thou the King of the Jews?', asked the Roman (John 18:33). Outwardly, he certainly did not appear regal, quite the reverse. Pilate had thoughts of the grandeur and magnificence he had seen in Rome, with the emperor looking every inch what he claimed to be. Jesus was merely a condemned prisoner, yet he possessed a serene nobility which shone through the façade, and he even answered the question as no prisoner would normally have dared. He questioned the interrogator! (John 18:34).

Jesus was careful to make the pagan procurator understand the nature of his kingship. Had he replied that he was a king, Pilate would have presumed him guilty of treason; on the other hand, he was certainly a king — the King of all kings. The governor looked genuinely puzzled. At least he was prepared to discuss the issue, which was not his usual custom with Jews brought for judgement.

It is often difficult, at times impossible, for a Christian to explain spiritual matters to someone whose thinking rises no higher than the earth. On one occasion, Jesus reminded the unbelieving Jews of this fact by telling them they were 'from beneath' and of this world, whereas he was from 'above' and not of this world (John 8:23). The two belong to different realms, have little in common. How much more so was this true of Jesus, whose purity was divine, in conversation with one familiar with the fleshpots of Rome!

In the hall were two who stood on opposite sides of the eternal divide: the Lord of glory and the representative of pagan Rome. They belonged to separate kingdoms, both noted for their different kinds of glory and beauty and both of whose kings were worshipped. For one brief morning they stood facing each other. Could there be any hope, albeit for a few seconds, of bridging the gulf between them?

Pilate must have appreciated that he was in an unusual situation, one from which his curiosity refused to shy away. When prisoners were brought to him for questioning, they felt the strength of his aggressive right hand. With Jesus he found himself offering a sensitive right ear! His prisoner was gaining an advantage over him; quietly but surely, the governor was being introduced to something new and outside his experience and training. Jesus had a way of approaching sinners and gaining their interest, even those as far removed from God as Pilate, a way of building bridges, however flimsy, and seeking to find some common ground. He employed a similar approach with a Samaritan woman, although with more encouraging results (John 4:5-30).

There were two matters which appealed to every Roman: the glory of the empire fortified by the might of military conquest. The sight of Roman generals proudly marching ahead of their conquering legions illustrated this. On the first 'Good Friday' morning Rome was at the zenith of her power, the Eternal City on the Tiber boasting pomp and splendour, with all roads throughout the known world literally leading to Cæsar's front door. He was the master, or so he and his subjects and slaves thought, of each of those roads and of every traveller upon them. He claimed deity as his right, and the citizens of the empire were required to offer incense to him as a mark of their allegiance. To be a Roman citizen, as the apostle Paul appreciated, was considered an honour for which men were prepared to pay (Acts 16:37-38; 22:27-28) There was no other kingdom to match the Roman empire, yet Pilate's prisoner not only claimed to know of one, but was its King!

Upon being asked what he had done to warrant arrest, Jesus almost casually introduced into the conversation the reality of his kingdom: 'My kingdom is not of this world' (John 18:36). To any Roman citizen, especially one of high rank, life was precarious and likely to be short. If there were not battles to be fought in the field, there were rivals to be noted. Cæsar particularly had to be on his guard against the potential assassin; therefore thoughts had to be constantly focused upon this world, not on any other.

However despite this, Pilate's interest was maintained when Jesus astonished him by adding, 'If my kingdom were of this world, then would my servants fight, that I should not be delivered to the Jews: but now is my kingdom not from hence' (John 18:36). He was graciously excusing Peter's violent behaviour in the garden, about which Pilate would have been told by the officer in charge of the temple guards. If caught Peter faced execution.

Pilate may have overlooked the apology in favour of another aspect of Jesus' remark, one which he could readily understand. What sort of king can control a kingdom without employing an army? Surely every kingdom needs one. Pilate could not conceive of the empire without its legions, or of Cæsar without his praetorium guard to protect him from the assassin's sword. Yet his prisoner was claiming to be the King of such a kingdom, one which was not of this world. He was losing the gist of what Jesus was telling him, and also his patience, but at that stage of the interrogation his bewilderment had not turned to outright hostility. 'Art thou a king then?', he asked with perhaps less incredulity than at the first (John 18:37).

'What is truth?'

At this point, Jesus had brought the governor to the moment where a personal decision on his part was called for and where there was a need to enter further into the discussion. Pilate had asked three questions about Jesus' person. Was he going to be drawn into asking about his mission? In other words, was he concerned enough about his soul to enquire after the nature of the gospel? It was in every way his 'moment of truth'. Yes Jesus was a King: 'To this end was I born, and for this cause came I into the world, that I should bear witness unto the truth. Everyone that is of the truth heareth my voice' (John 18:37).

Truth by its very nature is something desirable and worth attaining, but to find it men have sought long and hard throughout their entire lives. Where within the empire could Pilate lay hold of it — through the writings of the Greek and Roman philosophers or in the greatness of her art? Rome prided herself upon stern discipline, the rule of law and the pacifying of her numerous gods, and these were considered sufficient to unite her citizens and maintain the empire for generations to come.

Even Greece, famed as it was for its love of beauty and wisdom, did not possess truth (1 Cor. 1:22). All the prevailing philosophies were debated; all the existing art forms found expression in Athens, the 'university' of the ancient world. Travellers passing through, as Paul was (Acts 17:16-31), were invariably waylaid by the learned men and invited to share with them aspects of their culture and philosophy. For the Athenian philosophers, scraping among the ashes of other men's thoughts was among their chief delights. Indeed, in their search for truth Paul discovered they spent 'their time in nothing else, but either to tell, or to hear some new thing'

(Acts 17:21). It was fundamentally a religious act, denoting a feverish attempt at finding the correct answers to the questions all men ask in their yearning 'deep down' for reality.

Mankind originated from a common source, from which it has been cut off and to which it inwardly hankers to return. There is no possibility of rest and peace until it does so. In the meantime man clutches hold of intellectual straws in an effort to help him in his search. It is not a thirst for mere knowledge, but rather an innate longing for reality, for personal identity, which no one in his heart believes will ever be satisfied. Insoluble questions are always plentiful, but answers are never found. Consequently, there is a crying for satisfaction without finding it, and an endless hankering for peace without ever experiencing it.

As for the Jews, Pilate might have wondered whether Caiaphas and his fellow priests had discovered truth. They would certainly have thought so; after all, they were numbered among those to whom had been 'committed the oracles of God' (Rom. 3:2), and also '... the adoption, and the glory, and the covenants' (Rom. 9:4). Surely, of all people, the descendants of the patriarchs, the men to whom God revealed himself, knew the truth. In fact the tragedy was that although they could claim a racial kinship with Abraham and were legally bound to the covenant, they were not necessarily his 'children' in the sense of sharing the same saving faith (Gal. 3:9). As Paul put it, 'They are not all Israel, which are of Israel' (Rom. 9:6). In other words, despite all their privileges the Jewish nation did not possess the truth, but only certain aspects of it.

This debate had featured prominently in the controversial ministries of both John the Baptist and Jesus. They insisted that the Jews were unsaved, that their boasting was vain. God had taken hold of an axe and had, in Christ, hacked down the Jewish tree at the roots (Luke 3:9). Something new had begun and all reliance upon the Abrahamic covenant for salvation was null and void, with God demanding repentance and 'good fruit' to prove it (Matt. 7:13-29). In fact, and this enraged the Jews more than anything, there was no difference in God's sight between them and the hated Gentiles! Neither could boast in the possession of truth, whether through pagan philosophy or in formal religion. In the light of this Pilate's famous question, 'What is truth?', provides fresh vigour for the search.

Truth has its source in the mind of God, and can only be known and understood if he desires to reveal it. He would have been fully justified in leaving man to grope in the darkness, but instead he graciously manifested the truth by sending his Son to the world. That is why John the apostle was able to testify, 'Grace and truth came by Jesus Christ' (John 1:17). His remarkable prologue (John 1:1-18) reveals how this was accomplished. The divine Word came in order to communicate *the* truth — not just any truth or truths in general, but the ultimate in truth. He was 'full of grace and truth' (John 1:14). He insisted that he had 'proceeded forth and came from God', that his doctrine was not his own, 'but his that sent me' (John 7:16). The Speech, or Word, arrived in the midst of men in order to communicate the thoughts and feelings of the Father (John 14:6). He alone can supply the answers, all of which are found within 'the counsel of God' (Acts 20:27). Every true follower of Jesus has heard the voice of truth, and obeys it (3 John 3-4).

It was too much for Pilate. Not wishing to hear any more, he shrugged his shoulders: 'What is truth?' (John 18:38). It was not the question of a genuine enquirer, but one which revealed careless indifference and without waiting for an answer he returned to the Sanhedrin in the porch outside. Jesus was taken out with him.

Truth had spoken to Pilate face to face, but tragically, like most people, he failed to appreciate it. The question Jesus had asked the Jews on one occasion was equally applicable to the Roman governor, as was the answer he gave: 'Why do ye not understand my speech? Even because ye cannot hear my word' (John 8:43). They spoke the same language, could hold an intelligent conversation with each other, but by no means breathed the same heavenly air. Christ's 'word' is heaven's dialect, and it cannot be taught in any language school; a new and spiritual birth is required (John 3:7). It takes more than good eyesight to see the truth, and yet one can be physically deaf and still hear it if one has been born again.

Outside, the relative quietness of the hall was in sharp contrast to the noise of the gathering crowds on the pavement. In the porch

Jesus was met with verbal abuse as Caiaphas and his priests shouted accusations at him, but he remained silent. Pilate was amazed. Jesus had held a lengthy conversation with him, a Roman pagan, but was silent before his fellow Jews. His prisoner baffled him: 'Answerest thou nothing? Behold, how many things they witness against thee' (Mark 15:4). But the silence continued, for truth is not only revealed; it is at times kept hidden (1 Cor. 2:7-8).

The case is referred to Herod

By this time the people, realizing Pilate and Jesus were in the porch with the priests, directed their attention to the group above the steps. Pilate turned to them and pointing to his prisoner shouted out within hearing of both the priests and the people, 'I find no fault in this man' (Luke 23:4; John 18:38), a verdict guaranteed to produce an enraged outcry from the Sanhedrin. The priests were shocked, and tried again to change Pilate's mind by reminding him of Jesus' supposed guilt of insurrection, 'from Galilee to this place' (Luke 23:5).

Mention of Galilee came as a relief to Pilate, who by this time was sandwiched between the guile of the Sanhedrin and the gullibility of the crowds. When he heard that Jesus was from Galilee he saw a loophole through which he might escape from his responsibility. It so happened that Herod Antipas, the notorious son of an infamous father, was in Jerusalem on a visit. Herod had been tetrarch of Galilee since his father Herod the Great had died thirty years or so earlier. Pilate saw his chance to hand Jesus over to someone else.

It satisfied Herod's pride to think that Pilate had asked him to sit in judgement upon so famous a prisoner, especially as up till then they had been enemies. The fact that Pilate was merely using Herod for his own ends was conveniently overlooked, and instead the incident brought the two closer together (Luke 23:12).

Through the narrow streets Jesus was taken for the second stage of his civil trial towards Herod Antipas' residence, which may have been the Asmonean palace, once the home of the old Herodian family when in Jerusalem. It was a long and noisy procession, with

Jesus attended by the guards on either side of him and several dozen priests of the Sanhedrin, followed by the inquisitive crowds.

The procession no doubt lengthened as bystanders joined themselves to it. Soon the palace was the centre of attention as hundreds converged upon it and awaited events. Jesus was taken inside to meet the king who he had once been warned wanted to kill him. Jesus' comment on that occasion was revealing for it was the only time he had shown contempt for any single individual: 'Go ... and tell that fox, Behold, I cast out devils, and I do cures today and tomorrow, and the third day I shall be perfected' (Luke 13:31-32). Herod had to learn that assassination was not in the Father's plan and purpose for his Son. In other words, whatever Herod had planned for him was irrelevant. As the early church was later to pray, 'Herod, and Pontius Pilate, with the Gentiles, and the people of Israel, were gathered together, for to do whatsoever thy hand and thy counsel determined before to be done' (Acts 4:27-28).

The first time Herod Antipas had heard of Jesus and his miraculous powers, being superstitious he had immediately thought of John the Baptist. Perhaps the fiery preacher had risen from the dead to haunt him! (Luke 9:7-9). It had been he who had ordered the arrest and execution of John after his courageous denunciation of Herod's adultery, following the latter's marriage to his stepbrother Philip's wife (Luke 3:19-20).

The king was excited at the prospect of seeing Jesus. Perhaps he would perform a miracle in front of him (Luke 23:8). Such was the restless spirit of monarchs in ancient times that payment was made to anyone who could invent new and exciting pleasures. Herod's desire to meet Jesus was on that level: a wish to be entertained. He was disappointed, for although he tried hard Antipas failed to get his captive to open his mouth throughout the entire period they were together.

It was an ominous silence. Jesus had at least granted an opportunity for Pilate, the Roman eagle, to quest after salvation, but no chance was afforded for Herod, the Edomite fox (Gen. 36:1). Any 'birthright' that might have been his had long since been bartered (Gen. 25:29-34).

There being no miraculous spectacle to watch, the king plied his victim with questions. Nobody knows today what they were, but their absence from the scriptural record appears to suggest they were trivial and merely a substitute for Jesus' lack of entertainment value. Perhaps the fox was hoping he might be able to extract more information from the Lamb than the eagle had done. It would have been a boost to his ego to have been able to boast that he had.

Nothing produces rage from bullies more than a dignified silence. Herod's court suddenly erupted with the blare of angry voices as the priests, allowed in to share in what was to have been Herod's moment of triumph, shouted their repeated accusations against Jesus (Luke 23:10). They were not rebuked, but rather encouraged to vent their ire upon the victim by the king's own unregal behaviour. Jesus, the Lamb before his shearers, remained 'dumb' (Isa. 53:7). Herod also was infuriated. He had dealt with John the Baptist, an experience which had given him an uneasy conscience, and now he feared Jesus' reaction.

Nothing that he said to his prisoner appeared to ruffle him. He had wanted miracles, had asked questions, had listened to the priests' provocation: all to no avail. Mockery of the one claiming kingship was the last resort. Herod's father had sought to kill Jesus when newly-born, but had failed (Matt. 2:1-16). Now, in one of history's great ironies, the son of a king had the man born to be King at his mercy.

Mockery is the coward's last resort (Luke 23:11). Herod, aided by his guards, roughly handled Jesus, who was still bound with twine, and draped him in a sumptuous regal robe no doubt removed from Herod's shoulders. Thus fittingly attired as a king, Jesus silently suffered the taunts of all in the room. No mercy was expected by him, and none was shown. He who had known eternal purity in the highest, was now the butt of impure humanity at its lowest. He who had experienced exquisite and eternal love as God the Son was now subjected to vile hatred among the godless (John 17:24).

Herod, reflecting the depravity of his family, sought to convert the Christ into a clown while the priests cast aside their masks of piety and revelled in the devilish charade. The room was filled with coarse laughter as those claiming Jacob for their ancestor joined forces with the descendants of Esau to make merry with the Prince of peace. The messianic King-Priest saw the irony in it all as the Herodian king and Jewish high priest encouraged the obscenity (Zech. 6:13).

Jesting cannot survive for long without encouragement from the victim. Soon it must run its course and fizzle out in uneasiness and embarrassment. So it proved that morning. Jesus had failed to stimulate the excitement as he 'endured such contradiction of sinners against himself' (Heb. 12:3).

It was time for him to be sent on his way again, back to Pilate (Luke 23:11). Along the street Jesus was pulled unceremoniously by the rope around his neck to the Castle of Antonia. He was exhausted, not having closed his eyes for many hours, and his appearance must have begun to show it. He had been abused at the hands of the Jews, the Romans and now the Herodians. The strain was tremendous.

Making matters worse was the gruelling heat, increasing in intensity as the sun rose in an azure sky, as well as the jostling crowds on either side of him as they sought to obtain a good view of the proceedings. They had not witnessed anything like this before.

6.
The washing of the hands

It seemed as if all Jerusalem had arrived outside Antonia Castle. Pilate had heard them coming from a distance and was waiting in the porch, a throne-like chair having been brought out and placed into position. Jesus was taken up the flight of steps to join him. Everyone knew, including the governor, that not only was a decision expected from him but one which would satisfy the Sanhedrin. The members were probably assembled menacingly on the steps midway between him and the crowds. He was caught up in the web of intrigue and knew he was unable to extricate himself.

When the noise had abated sufficiently for him to be heard, Pilate pointed to Jesus and made his unpopular declaration to all assembled: 'I find in him no fault at all.' A cry ascended from an increasingly hostile audience, the people by this time mouthing the desires of the priests. Pilate managed to quieten them again, and produced what he thought was a likely solution: 'But ye have a custom, that I should release unto you one at the passover...' (John 18:38-39). He was in a quandary. His interrogation of the prisoner had convinced him there was 'something' about him, that he would need to be careful. If therefore he could remove the glare of publicity from Jesus to another he hoped his many critics would be pacified.

In custody not far away, as everyone knew, was a notorious individual named Barabbas, a thief, murderer and insurrectionist due to be crucified that day. Pilate saw his chance and took it: 'Whom will ye that I release unto you? Barabbas, or Jesus which is called Christ?' (Matt. 27:17). The question was barbed, for in seeking to draw away attention from Jesus Pilate also revealed his contempt for the Jews amassed before him. He knew that despite the Sanhedrin's pretence at piety, as has already been noted, envy was the motive behind their hatred of Jesus and that the people were merely mouthing the official policy (John 11:49-53). He therefore gave them all a choice: they could choose between undisputed wickedness or innocent purity. Which was it to be? Surely, claiming the righteous Hebrew God as their own, they would not wish to opt for the former!

Pilate's wife intervenes

While Pilate's offer was being mooted a messenger was seen whispering in his ear. He had come from within the main building on behalf of Pilate's wife. Pilate appeared startled, if not somewhat annoyed, for Roman procurators were unused to interference from their spouses in matters concerning official business. Her name is not mentioned in Scripture, but history records that it was Claudia Procula. She had been woken that morning by the tumult on the pavement below, following a nightmare.

Evidently before retiring for the night her husband had mentioned that he was expecting a visit from the Sanhedrin in connection with Jesus of Nazareth. She had often heard his name mentioned, both within the castle and in society as a whole. It was not surprising that she should have dreamt about him, the one who was causing her husband so many problems.

The details of the disturbing dream are not known, but uppermost in her mind when she awoke was the fact that Jesus was righteous and therefore innocent of the charges levelled against him. Equally impressed upon her mind was the realization that her husband's involvement in the machinations of the Sanhedrin should end immediately and that he was being dragged into a situation from which it would be difficult or even impossible to escape. The message whispered to Pilate was clear: 'Have thou nothing to do with that just man: for I have suffered many things this day in a dream because of him' (Matt. 27:19).

Pilate was now under greater pressure. God the Son had graciously confronted him with the question of eternal values; now the Father was warning him through Claudia's dream. In effect the message given three years earlier at Jesus' baptism was heard again: 'This is my beloved Son, in whom I am well pleased' (Matt. 3:17), but Pilate had gone too far along this road to falter. Roman pride was at stake.

The New Testament reveals Pilate's dilemma and unease. Until that moment he had two parties opposing him — the priests and the people. Now a third one had arisen, and one much closer to him! Having listened to the messenger he knew a decision was called for, but what was it to be? The crowds were growing impatient, chanting Barabbas' name.

Pilate tries to pass the blame

Pilate suddenly realized what he had to do: shift the onus of blame from himself to the people. Which of the two would the crowds want released? (Matt. 27:21). Whatever they replied, he would feel obliged to concede to their wishes, and in this way would avoid the responsibility of following his conscience and setting Jesus free. The chanting continued from the steps and the pavement, everyone calling for Barabbas' release. Pilate felt relieved, but at the expense of knowing that, whereas the previous day he had believed himself to be a proud, self-confident Roman, he was now publicly exposed as a weak and dissolute man.

In the meantime, he continued to sidestep the governor's responsibility — one which he had exercised many times before — that of passing judgement upon the prisoner. It was unlikely that he had been so hesitant on the previous occasions. He decided to wriggle free from the ultimate decision and allow majority thinking to have its way, a practice seldom indulged in by Roman officials: 'What shall I do then with Jesus which is called Christ...' (Matt. 27:22)

'...whom ye call the King of the Jews?' (Mark 15:12). They had no hesitation in voicing an opinion, a roar ascending from all sides: 'Let him be crucified.'

Pilate felt his guilt-ridden dilemma slipping away. After all, if he was so outnumbered what else could he do but comply with the majority? Then came the *coup de grâce*. Pilate, having apparently shifted all blame from himself, created the impression that he was supportive of Jesus: 'Why, what evil hath he done?' (Matt. 27:23). Everyone would be satisfied, including his wife, and not least his conscience, that the condemnation of Jesus had been a democratic decision. As far as he was concerned, he had publicly upheld Jesus' innocence. Jesus, standing nearby, was the only one not deceived.

As the chanting, 'Let him be crucified' (Matt. 27:22), reached a crescendo Pilate sought the ultimate loophole in seeking to be justified in the eyes of the Sanhedrin and the state, and not least of Jesus himself. They all had to be made aware that he was exonerated of all personal blame in the matter. In fact he had to be *seen* to be innocent; words can get lost in the chaos of such an occasion.

Pilate ordered a servant, perhaps Claudia's who was still close by, to fetch a bowl, some water and a towel. Once these items appeared the ignoble Roman ostentatiously rinsed his hands in the water making sure all eyes were upon him. Surely they would believe him now as he said, 'I am innocent of the blood of this just person', and then to underline his apparent nobility of character and motive he added, 'See *ye* to it' (Matt. 27:24). They did. In the most notorious decision of history, Barabbas was freed. Then, surely to the astonishment of even the hardened Pilate, and in a way which underlined the satanic element in the entire proceedings, those baying for Jesus' death screamed forth an alarming oath: 'His blood be on us, and on our children' (Matt. 27:25). Jesus was scourged in full view of them all.

The scourging

The scourging was always the preliminary to crucifixion. It was recognized as being an extremely brutal way of administering punishment and no Roman citizen was allowed by law to receive it (Acts 16:37). Many strong men died as a result; most would have fainted. The victim was stripped to the waist and tied in a bent position to a post, so that his back was taut and well exposed. Then two powerfully built men ('lictors'), standing on either side of him, delivered the blows in quick succession. They carried whips with leather thongs, each one weighted with jagged edges of bone or lead, and as each blow was struck the pieces dug deeply into the flesh. Soon open wounds crisscrossed the back and rivulets of blood oozed freely from them, until it dripped from the flesh hanging like ribbons. At times when the sufferer twisted and flinched in agony, the thongs failed to find their target and instead curled over the shoulders or around the head.

There is no record of how many blows Jesus received, nor is it important for anyone to know, but the customary number would have made it difficult for him to stand up, let alone walk. Yet he and the two thieves who later joined him were obliged to do both when his ordeal was partially over, for once the soldiers had cut Jesus down from the whipping post they gratified their bestiality further. Pilate did not order fresh cruelties, but he must have known what the men might wish to do to his suffering prisoner.

The soldiers mock Jesus

As the crowds awaited fresh developments, they watched as Jesus was goaded by his guards, half standing and half crawling, into the main building. There, out of sight, more soldiers joined the guards as together they too waited for the governor to declare his verdict from the porch. They decided to amuse themselves by forcing Jesus, the King of the Jews, to participate in a mock coronation. It formed part of a dice game popular with legionaries, the remains of which can still be seen scratched upon the cobble stones.

With ruffian hands they ripped off the remainder of their victim's clothing, until completely humiliated, he stood naked before the jeering onlookers. It says much for Jesus' physical strength that he could endure this continued cruelty without collapsing. Nearby there lay a soldier's scarlet mantle, a discarded one, for there was much blood on their victim's back and the owner would not have wanted his tunic soiled (Matt. 27:28). It served a useful purpose as a regal robe, although not as impressive a one as Herod's had been a short time before. They placed the mantle around Jesus' bruised and bloodied shoulders, and with a stick in his hand acting as a sceptre, the one who within weeks would be seated at God's right hand in glory (Heb. 1:3) was pushed into his 'throne' by Pilate's proud prætorium guard. The excruciating pain and nervous tension expressed themselves in his eyes.

Someone fetched a few twigs from a particularly thorny plant, and managed to twist it into the shape of a crown. The Romans were not fussy about how it should be worn; regardless of the pain inflicted they rammed it down on Jesus' head until the crown was wedged and the skin pierced. Fresh blood began to trickle, which prompted a frenzy of raucous delight. The King of an everlasting dominion, whom all other dominions will one day serve (Dan.7:14), endured such mockery from the lowly citizens of a decaying empire. The Word of God, whose fist contains the iron rod of divine judgement (Rev. 19:15), meekly submitted to the blows inflicted by hands covered in his blood. Their foul spittle marked the face of the one who holds the 'keys of hell and of death' (Rev. 1:18). It was a fearful irony.

The prophecy of Isaiah was not known to Jesus' tormentors, but it would have sprung to his mind: 'I gave my back to the smiters, and my cheeks to them that plucked off the hair. I hid not my face from shame and spitting. For the Lord God will help me; therefore shall not I be confounded: therefore have I set my face like a flint, and I know that I shall not be ashamed. He is near that justifieth me; who will contend with me? Let us stand together: who is mine adversary? Let him come near to me' (Isa. 50:6-8).

With the governor's approach, the soldiers ended their fun and games. Pilate, seeing what they had done to Jesus, made no effort to admonish them for their unruly behaviour; nor did he allow the prisoner a moment to recover himself and remove the objects of ridicule. Indeed, he intended to use Jesus as a visual aid to illustrate a point to the waiting crowds.

The presentation to the waiting crowd

Instead, Pilate went out to them, leaving behind him the beauty of unusual purity at the mercy of uncontrolled depravity. His mind was occupied with another matter: the justification of himself in the eyes of the people — and especially those of Cæsar in Rome. Glancing over his shoulder to estimate the emperor's thoughts was an occupational hazard. Once outside, he addressed the increasingly impatient multitude: 'Behold, I bring him forth to you, that ye may know that I find no fault in him' (John 19:4).

At that moment Jesus was seen walking very slowly through the porch from the judgement hall to the top of the steps. Many in the crowds must have been aware of the pathos behind his appearance; some would have been shocked by what they saw. He was in an obvious state of collapse following the hours of strain, culminating in the scourging he had received. The muscular figure who strode the length and breadth of Israel for three years, covering distances of seventy miles or more in a preaching tour, had been greatly weakened. The one who could heal multitudes last thing at night, and then rise to pray 'a great while before day' (Mark 1:32-35), in anticipation of many hours spent ministering was, physically, only a shadow of his former self.

This was an opportunity for the people to ask themselves why Jesus was treated so wickedly (Acts 2:23). In their hearts they would have agreed with Peter's assessment of his Lord, that 'God anointed Jesus of Nazareth with the Holy Ghost and with power: who went about doing good, and healing all that were oppressed of the devil; for God was with him' (Acts 10:38).

Many of them had joyfully followed him from Galilee as he made his way to Jerusalem for the passover feast (Luke 9:51). They could have testified to Jesus' words of comfort to an imprisoned and failing John the Baptist that 'The blind receive their sight, and the lame walk, the lepers are cleansed, and the deaf hear, the dead are raised up, and the poor have the gospel preached to them' (Matt. 11:5). Now here he was standing before them, a silent rebuke to their fickleness and disloyalty.

With a gesture towards Jesus, Pilate declared with a loud voice

to the entire assembly, '*Ecce homo!* Behold the man!' His contemptuous sneer reflected Rome's attitude towards physical weakness.
His prisoner might claim to be the King of an invisible kingdom, but
with his thorny crown and tattered bloodied mantle what a dismal
picture he painted! Besides, where were his armies? If they existed,
the King had told him they were not even prepared to go to war on
his behalf (John 18:36). How different from the might of Rome, with
Cæsar king of all he surveyed and his conquering armies encamped
throughout his extensive domains!

Three lessons for all time

Pilate's voice continues to reverberate, but this time around the
world, with Jesus still the centre of attraction and focal point for
discussion. The Roman empire officially came to an end in A. D.
476 when Rome fell to Odoacer the Herulean, but the kingdom of
God grows like the grain of mustard seed Jesus spoke about. It is
indeed 'the least of all seeds: but when it is grown, it is the greatest
among herbs, and becometh a tree, so that the birds of the air come
and lodge in the branches' (Matt. 13:32).

Early on that morning, as Jesus stood silently in front of his
accusers and abusers, three matters registered themselves in everyone's mind. These same factors need to be re-examined today by
fair-minded people. First was *the person of Jesus*, who although
faint with exhaustion and near to collapse nevertheless revealed an
unusual strength of character. The soldiers in particular would have
been aware of this had they stopped to reflect upon it. Throughout
their savage session with him Jesus had not once complained, nor
had he sought to retaliate, as they would have expected (1 Peter
2:23).

It was their custom to take advantage of their prisoners, to gain
pleasure from others' pain. Usually, the wretched victim fought and
cursed his tormentors with as much vigour as he could muster in the
circumstances. Jesus was not like that: he submitted himself to the
indignities and humiliation in complete resignation to the Father's
will and in loving submission to his enemies. In other words, Jesus

practised what he had preached to a remarkable degree: 'I say unto you, Love your enemies, bless them that curse you, do good to them that hate you, and pray for them which despitefully use you, and persecute you' (Matt. 5:44). How simple it is to preach from the text, but how difficult to practise it! The Sanhedrin would have been too biased against Jesus to have noted his gracious demeanour, but Pilate expressed amazement at it (Matt. 27:12-14).

If only they had been capable of reflecting upon what they had all witnessed! In close proximity to them stood the Light of the world, penetrating the darkness of heathenism and Jewish apostasy (John 12:46). As one who had volunteered at the Father's behest to suffer and die for sinners (John 3:16), however loathsome and vile, Jesus expected the treatment he had received. Indeed he had forewarned the disciples of the impending trauma (Matt. 16:21). Thus when it arrived he submitted in the spirit of gracious humility, which did not make the suffering less distressful but supplied a positive reason for it.

Then there was the grotesque irony of *the crown of thorns*. It had been thrust on Jesus' head in a gesture of defiance of all he claimed for himself and his kingdom. The anguish and pain it caused was immaterial to the scorners, and with its hasty manufacture Satan mocked the eternal crown of righteousness that the Lord of glory wears, as befits his exalted position upon the throne of his Father (Rev. 3:21).

That 'crown' still tantalizes, dividing mankind into three. There are those who stand alongside the Roman soldiers in their vilification of Jesus of Nazareth, who refuse to give credence to him or his teaching. For them Christianity rises no higher than the thorns which comprised the crown, and nothing will persuade them otherwise except the sovereign power of God. Theirs is a churlish unbelief, the reasons for which are found in the words of the rejected Jesus, that he and he alone is the light, but men naturally gravitate away from him towards the darkness for fear of the exposure of their sins (John 3:18-20). These are the 'dogs' by whom the holy things of God are likely to be defiled, the 'swine' insensitive to the preciousness of pearls (Matt. 7:6).

There are also those who, although sympathetic to Jesus, are undecided about him. They reject the cruelty and flagrant unbelief of both the pagans and the priests on that Friday morning, and acknowledge his evident innocence of the trumped-up charges levelled against him. However, for them the crown still hovers over his head, and they are unsure of its intrinsic value. They cannot make up their minds whether they see a genuine crown adorning his head, or just thorns. For the answer they must turn to Jesus himself, and to those who knew him intimately. In other words, there is a third view.

For example, John the Baptist at the River Jordan, just three years prior to the events at the fortress of Antonia, saw Jesus entering the water for baptism to mark the commencement of his ministry. John testified to the fact that he possessed no prior knowledge of Jesus' sonship with the Father (John 1:31), until he saw the sign that God had given him: 'Upon whom thou shalt see the Spirit descending, and remaining on him, the same is he which baptizeth with the Holy Ghost' (John 1:33). Once John saw 'the Spirit of God descending like a dove, and lighting upon him' (Matt.3:16), he had no hesitation in humbling himself before his cousin: 'I have need to be baptized of thee, and comest thou to me?' (Matt. 3:14). On that day when Jesus was baptized, publicly committing himself to his Father's will, everyone present heard a voice from heaven: 'This is my beloved Son, in whom I am well pleased' (Matt. 3:16-17). John was so convinced that he insisted: 'I saw, and bare record that this is the Son of God' (John 1:34).

The apostles walked closer to Jesus than John did, and saw remarkable evidences of his grace and glory; indeed they 'were eyewitnesses of his majesty' (2 Peter 1:16). They were not detached observers, but stood beside him every day for those famous three years and noted the miraculous powers he possessed, his divine utterances and, perhaps above everything else, the perfection of his character. They also saw him pinned to the cross, risen from the dead and triumphantly ascending back to his Father. If the unbelievers who heard Jesus said, 'Never man spake like this man' (John 7:46), the apostles were able to go one step further: 'We beheld his glory, the glory as of the only begotten of the Father, full of grace and truth' (John 1:14).

As for *the bedraggled robe* which was draped around Jesus' lacerated shoulders, that too has a message for each generation. It was beggarly, crumpled and soiled — for many an apt description of the Christian faith, which they believe has no more relevance than the discarded mantle, useful for a period but now outliving its time. They assume Christianity will eventually fade away, leaving behind it only a few strands of decaying tissue.

In fact such opinions are quaintly outmoded. Since the days of the early church men have hoped and believed that Jesus' influence and that of his people would evaporate (Acts 5:38-39). Two thousand years later the wish has still not been granted! Men and women persist in forsaking everything for Jesus, the Son of God, as readily as those fishermen on Galilee's shore (Mark 1:17). They do so because the robe, far from being yesterday's cast-off, is eternally glorious.

There is no finer material than Christ's robe of righteousness, made of 'fine linen, clean and white' (Rev. 19:8). During his days in the flesh that righteousness had been a puzzle to his critics, which is understandable in the light of man's natural inclination, yet Jesus alone held no qualms in challenging them, and when he enquired, 'Which of you convinceth me of sin?' nobody argued with him (John 8:46). It was evident to them that Jesus possessed a purity which was as unfathomable as it was unique. Pilate himself recognized something of this when interrogating his prisoner, and later confessed, 'I find no fault in him' (John 19:4).

The robe of righteousness completely covers the army of God (Rev. 19:14), each member of Christ's body the church (Col. 1:18). The frailest Christian is accepted by almighty God as being 'in Christ' (2 Cor. 5:17), whose righteousness is put to the believer's account (2 Cor. 5:21). One day the church of which he or she is a part will be brought to the royal court, 'not having spot, or wrinkle, or any such thing' — in fact 'holy and without blemish' (Eph. 5:27).

Pilate's continuing dilemma

'Behold the man!', shouted Pilate and the sight of Jesus so weakened and bedraggled enraged the Sanhedrin still further. With shouts of

'Crucify him, crucify him!' they made their intentions clear. Once more the onus was pushed towards the unwilling governor. Justifying himself was not proving straightforward for Pilate. Impatiently he tried to free himself from the situation, by suggesting Jesus should be handed back to the Jews to deal with. Still he insisted upon the prisoner's innocence, but Caiaphas and his fellow priests were too wily for him. They recognized a troubled man when they saw one.

All Judean governors feared a Jewish uprising in Jerusalem during the feasts. With so many excitable and passionate Jews confined within such a small circumference, the city was like a tinder-box and any uprising from the downtrodden people was likely to spark off the nation's resentment against Roman rule. Riots would follow and the noise and chaos would be heard in Rome, and if the emperor saw fit, Judea's governor would be summoned to answer. Romans felt strongly about law and order.

The Sanhedrin's belligerence, coupled with his wife's dream, caused Pilate to fear the worst, especially when he heard the words: 'We have a law, and by our law he ought to die, because he made himself the Son of God' (John 19:7-8). Pilate knew that unless he did something about the situation quickly it had all the marks of a potential catastrophe. The chief priests, supported by the weight of their authority, together with Jerusalem overflowing with passionate Jews ready to listen to them, were not to be trifled with.

Once again Jesus was ordered to follow Pilate into the judgement hall, the troubled procurator probably thinking he would be able to assess the situation more clearly if he interrogated his prisoner yet again. Something he said might provide a solution. Pilate appeared more of a prisoner than did Jesus, who, despite the horrendous marks of scourging, dictated the terms of the interrogation. While he chose to speak, or to remain silent, his captor paced to and fro from the Sanhedrin in the porch to Jesus in the hall like a man pacing a cell. Somehow or another Pilate was determined to rid himself of this crisis, but he was baffled about how to do it. In an attempt at discovering an answer he demanded to know from Jesus who and what he was, and where he had come from. But Jesus' silence this time only made matters worse for him (John 19:9-10).

Pilate appeared almost frantic. He was trapped by the San-hedrin's strong hint of a possible uprising, his wife's unnerving persistence and Jesus' claims of deity. It was uncanny, but the condemned prisoner was the only one who could help him. He *must* speak! He almost pleaded with Jesus to say something, reminding him of his powers as a Roman official to do with him as he desired. Surely, the realization that he might be freed if he co-operated would be sufficient for Jesus to help himself. Everyone does in a crisis.

Whatever answer Pilate expected he was shocked by the one he received: 'Thou couldest have no power at all against me, except it were given thee from above' (John 19:11). Jesus had been silent in Herod's presence, but Pilate was allowed a second opportunity to hear the truth. The kingdom over which Jesus reigns is not only greater than any other, including the Roman empire, but sovereignly orders their affairs. Before Pilate could reply to this astonishing claim his prisoner added, 'Therefore he that delivered me unto thee hath the greater sin' (John 19:11).

His kingdom governs universally, but also personally. It is concerned with private morals as well as public office. The kingdom of heaven is the arbiter over all nations and peoples, Jews, Gentiles, rich and poor (Isa. 40:18-23). In short, despite his appearance and attire as a condemned prisoner, he was both organizer and judge of the entire proceedings! The fickle crowds, the priestly hypocrites, the vile Herod, the faltering governor — they were all pawns on his giant chessboard.

Pilate had nothing to say, such was his bewilderment, but he listened with more than a passing interest, for 'from thenceforth' he tried every way he could to have Jesus released (John 19:12). He immediately returned to the porch seeking an opportunity, but the several dozen priests proved too great an obstacle to whatever good intentions he might have had. It appears he suggested Jesus could be released; after all, he had been scourged and that was surely punishment enough. The surly priests were in no mood to be convinced and refused to let him off the hook. If he set Jesus free, who claimed to be a king, what would Cæsar say? Surely Pilate was not suggesting the emperor had a legitimate rival! The thought horrified Pilate, for he understood what happened to those accused of treason.

He was trapped in a cul-de-sac of indecision, obliged to align himself publicly with either Cæsar or Jesus, a situation politicians find themselves in today. In a state of continued agitation Pilate once again returned to the judgement hall to fetch Jesus, who by this time must have been in a state of complete exhaustion. As well as the scourging, he had not rested or scarcely sat down since the previous evening. It was still early in the morning but the heat was beginning to stifle, and his sufferings, far from being over, had scarcely begun.

Pilate's final appeal to the crowds

Yet again Pilate took Jesus back to the porch, the governor sitting and the prisoner remaining on his feet (John 19:13-14). Several hours had passed since the Sanhedrin first arrived at Antonia. Now everyone knew the final decision was about to be made. Pilate was careful not to create the impression that he associated with Jesus, or that he sided with the Jewish priests either; at the same time he recognized the relevance of his wife's dream. He even attempted to appease Jesus and his claims. In short, he tried to please everyone and ended by pleasing no one. Not long before he had declared, 'Behold the man!' This time he changed the appeal to 'Behold *your* King!' Jesus was not his king, but theirs.

The Sanhedrin stamped their feet. They too wished to distance themselves from Jesus. Vehemently the priests persisted in their chanting: 'Away with him, away with him!' Pilate wished to make it clear once more that he disowned his prisoner, and at the same time could not resist taunting these hypocritical enemies of both God and Rome. 'Shall I crucify your *King*?' he shouted, but in replying the Sanhedrin exposed their unbelief: 'We have no king but Cæsar' (John 19:15). In their determination to resist Jesus' claims, this treacherous body of religious leaders publicly rejected their Sovereign God whom they claimed to serve. Their hatred for his Son had shattered the mask. In the meantime, Barabbas paced his cell.

7.
The quest for freedom

During the feast days when Jerusalem was overflowing, the cells within the fortress of Antonia were likely to have had a number of occupants. Policing the city was a difficult task, with the Roman militia hard-pressed to keep control over a wide cross-section of humanity. Many and varied were the crimes committed on such occasions, but the one which caused the most problems when it arose was the rioting generated by the Jewish resentment of the Roman occupation of the land, and especially Jerusalem itself.

The Jews, whose exiled ancestors had wept when they remembered the city, and had vowed, 'If I forget thee, O Jerusalem, let my right hand forget her cunning ... if I prefer not Jerusalem above my chief joy' (Ps. 137:5-6), were not going to forgive the Gentile aliens whose presence desecrated all they held dear. The fact that the fortress was situated so near the temple, the focal point of the festive activities, only aggravated their grievances. A Roman shadow was cast across its precincts, and in the event of any trouble, soldiers were able to rush down the flight of steps which linked it to the Tower of Antonia and quell the disturbances within minutes. The culprits were brusquely dragged to the cells. Once there, they were inside Roman territory without help from outside and at the mercy of their captors.

The cells were not intended to provide comfort for the prisoners; the thickness of the walls and the sturdiness of the bars were the only considerations. In the dank atmosphere, the incarcerated possessed little hope and no possibility of escape. The fortress swarmed with Roman legionaries, like ants in an anthill, and sentries efficiently guarded all the gates. The prisoners' only occupation was to await their fate at the governor's discretion, and dream of better times.

Barabbas, the popular hero

On the Friday morning, an occupant of one of the cells was destined to play a central role in the dramatic events taking place not far away. The Scriptures call him Barabbas. This was not his actual name, but merely a useful title. He was 'Bar-Abbas', the son of Abbas, although the interesting theory that his father was a prominent rabbi has no basis in fact. Nor has the story which circulated centuries later, that he too was called Jesus! Nevertheless, although he had killed someone during an uprising, he was no ordinary criminal, as subsequent events were to reveal (Mark 15:7).

No one knows what thoughts were passing through his mind when he was pushed into the cell to await his fate. He had been charged with the most serious of crimes: sedition and murder (Luke 23:19) and also robbery (John 18:40). Execution could be the only outcome. He knew he would soon be taken from his cell to face the judicial scourging, and then made to carry his cross to Calvary amidst the tumult caused by excited mobs and the lashes from Roman whips. He also appreciated that, as a rebel against the occupational forces, he would be the special target for the expression of Roman fury. Yet Barabbas had the satisfaction of knowing that beyond the confines of Antonia in the streets of Jerusalem he was a hero in the eyes of his fellow Jews (Matt. 27:16) He had dared to shake his fist at the Roman eagle.

His countrymen were united in their fervent hatred of Gentile foreigners who trampled upon their land, people and culture. Jewish men yearned to do something about the situation, but few were prepared to risk their lives in the attempt. They had been reared on facts and legends about their national hero, Judas Maccabæus, the 'hammer' of Israel. Every Jewish boy had learned of Judas' courageous and daring exploits, and no doubt wished one day to emulate his feats. Barabbas was no exception, but unlike most of his contemporaries, his dreams were at least partially realized.

The heroic uprising, so much a part of Jewish folklore and that which had inspired Barabbas, began nearly two hundred years prior to his arrest, in 168 B.C. The Syrian king, Antiochus 'Epiphanes', decided to destroy the Jewish religion. His armies conquered Israel and desecrated the temple in Jerusalem. Religious sacrifices, the possession of the law, sabbath-keeping and circumcision were forbidden and disobedience to these restrictions was a capital offence. Instead, the Olympian Zeus was set up in the temple, and all Jews were commanded to offer pagan sacrifices upon the altars erected by Antiochus' men.

The Jews did not suffer such indignities for long. An old priest, Mattathias, refused to sacrifice as commanded. Furthermore, he killed a compromising Jew as well as a Syrian officer nearby. This act sparked off a raging fire between the Jews and the conquering Syrians. Mattathias, with his seven sons, one of whom was Judas, fled to the hills crying out, 'Whosoever is zealous of the law, follow me!' They were joined by many others of like mind. The Maccabæan Revolt had begun. When the old priest died, his son Judas was declared leader. He was called 'Makkabi', or 'hammer', and as such became one of the most charismatic guerilla leaders of all time. The rest is history, and it explains why Barabbas sought to emulate his example.

The cell block was a hive of gossip, as each fresh prisoner brought the latest news with him. This time the chatter was about Jesus of Nazareth. The famous prophet and miracle-worker had been arrested. Soon, he would be joining them in the cells. The previous evening confirmed the rumour for there had been much activity within the city, and the sound of marching as a contingent of temple guards had been involved in the arrest.

Barabbas and his fellow prisoners, including two thieves also awaiting crucifixion, would have had a secret regard for Jesus. They would have heard of his association with people of their kind, the 'publicans and sinners', and have known how popular he was with them (Luke 15:1-2). It was evident that Jesus was sympathetic towards such people, if not to their sinful way of life, at least to their plight. Without excusing their behaviour, Jesus recognized that these poor people were victims of the politico-religious system

which had reared them. He went out of his way to show them love
and pity, to socialize with them and listen to their grievances.

The people's grievances

They had many, the greatest being that Israel lay in bondage.
Everyone agreed about this, except for a few proud and bitter Jews
(John 8:33). Tyranny loomed large over the nation and it appeared
that nothing could be done about the situation. Rome ruled with a
rod of iron, from her vassals in high places to the soldiers on every
street corner and at every gate. What made it worse was the pleasure
she took in degrading the downtrodden people. As already noted,
Pilate was particularly notorious for this. His cruelty was infamous,
and perpetrated with equal venom in the south as well as the north
of the land.

The New Testament supplies an incident of Pilate's vindictive
hatred for the Jews, one that took place in Galilee. During religious
festivities his troops had massacred some of the worshippers. Not
content with that, he went to the trouble of commanding the soldiers
to sacrilegiously mingle the victims' blood with the sacrificial
offerings (Luke 13:1). It was not surprising that the Jews desired the
overthrow of the repressive regime, and that Barabbas and others
were prepared to retaliate in an equally vicious manner.

What made matters worse was the inability of the people to trust
their religious leaders. Invariably, a distressed nation under the yoke
of oppression believes that if everything else is wrong in the land at
least it can turn to God's representatives. The Jews did not have that
opportunity. On the one hand, the Sadducees were obligated to the
Romans who had favoured them. The aristocrats and the wealthy
came very largely from this group, and therefore they had benefited
greatly from the political situation. In any case, as we have seen, the
Sadducean party had been selected by the Gentile foreigners as
custodians of Jewish temple worship, and even the office of high
priest was a Roman appointment.

The Jews did not receive any encouragement from the Pharisees
either. Despite the hatred they shared for the Roman conquerors,

needless to say Barabbas and the Pharisees had nothing in common and would not have come into contact with each other. The word 'Pharisee' reveals why: it means the 'separate one'. The only fellowship a Pharisee enjoyed was with his own kind. In any case, by the time of Christ it was impossible to distinguish between their love for the law and their worship of God. As for those like Barabbas and the 'publicans and sinners', who broke the laws of God and the traditional embellishments of rabbinical tradition with impunity, a Pharisee loathed them as much as he did the Gentile Romans (Luke 18:10-14). To whom, then, could the Jews go if not to the Sanhedrin?

John the Baptist heralds the ministry of Jesus

Suddenly, there appeared a chink of light in their dismal circumstances. A man called John with remarkable powers began preaching in Judæa (Luke 1:17). Multitudes streamed to hear him alongside the River Jordan (Matt. 3:5). On the one hand, he echoed the prevailing national discontentment by openly challenging Cæsar's vassal, Herod Antipas, about his scandalous behaviour which was well known to all (Mark 6:16-27). On the other, he heralded the arrival in Israel of a new era with the dramatic words: 'And now also the axe is laid unto the root of the trees: every tree therefore which bringeth not forth good fruit is hewn down, and cast into the fire' (Luke 3:9). To those of Barabbas' persuasion, in one blow he appeared to be denouncing both the Romans and the Sanhedrin. At the same time, John made it plain that the long-awaited Messiah had arrived, indeed was somewhere in the crowds standing on the banks of the Jordan (John 1:26). The frustrated Jews, so long oppressed, began to believe that at last their political problems would soon be at an end.

It was not long before John the Baptist's effective ministry came to the attention of the Sanhedrin in Jerusalem. Representatives were sent to question the preacher, whose appearance was strange and reminiscent of another age (John 1:19-28). They wished to know whether he considered himself the Messiah, no doubt in the hope of effecting an arrest should he claim to be so. John was able to assure his questioners that he was not claiming greatness for himself. Rather, he was only fulfilling the prophecy of Isaiah and ushering in the Messiah (Isa. 40:3).

Barabbas must have observed the national fervour with growing interest, especially after John's arrest and imprisonment by Herod's men. Then, what had at first appeared a slim hope quickly developed into a bright beam of light. Jesus made his presence felt throughout Israel and beyond. On both sides of the Jordan, and even in Syria, his fame spread like wildfire (Matt. 4:24-25). Vast crowds followed him, and mysterious and miraculous occurrences were reported. Jesus was evidently someone to be noted if Judaism was to be delivered.

What would have been equally clear to Barabbas was that although Jesus made no attempt to oppose Rome, he was certainly not a collaborator like the Sadducees (Mark 12:17). Even more evident was his distrust of the Sanhedrin itself. Rumours spread, which Barabbas would have heard, of the public disagreements between Jesus and the priests. Jesus' condemnation of them was known to all, and the fact that he blamed them for the existing malaise in Israel. They were the 'plants' which his Father would pull up by the roots, the 'blind guides' leading the blind into ditches (Matt. 15:13-14). There was also the astonishing display of indignation when he swept from the temple the market vendors whose livelihoods had been secured by the Sadducees (John 2:12-17).

Barabbas would have been very attracted by what he thought was Jesus' general approach to the existing situation in Israel. Here was a man after his own heart! However, he was to be disillusioned, as were some of Jesus' disciples who saw themselves, as did James and John, occupying important posts within the governing of a restored and triumphant Israel (Matt. 20:20-22). The disciples, reflecting the prevailing teaching, thought that 'the kingdom of God should immediately appear' (Luke 19:11).

But after three years of ministering to the people, Jesus still had not attempted to overthrow the establishment. The result of his entry into Jerusalem, with the waving palms and excited anticipation, must have proved as much a disappointment to Barabbas as it was to the disciples. Had the prophet not told of a day when, amid great rejoicing, 'Thy King cometh ... riding upon an ass...'? (Zech. 9:9). Yet apart from a skirmish in the temple and the noisy crowds shouting their expectancy, he still refrained from raising an army and ascending to the throne. He even allowed himself to be arrested without a struggle, with Peter's attempt at resistance being rebuked by Jesus for violent behaviour. Barabbas and many others were bewildered. The glory of Israel was at stake! Like the two men who walked the Emmaus road soon afterwards, Barabbas had undoubtedly 'trusted that it had been he which should have redeemed Israel' (Luke 24:21).

The true liberty Christ came to bring

Of course, Jesus' failure to please both Rome and the Jewish leaders in no way implied any agreement on his part with the nationalistic spirit so prevalent in Israel. In fact, far from liberating the people from political tyranny, Jesus made it plain that he believed they were in greater bondage than they realized, a bondage much more tyrannical than that of Rome. Satan was in possession of their souls; they were his children (John 8:44); and it was from these chains Jesus desired to liberate mankind. If the people responded they would experience the greatest liberty of all (John 8:32,36). This was surely the point at which Barabbas and his kind would have turned away.

The Sadducees also had little contact with Jesus, apart from one or two isolated incidents, such was their unbelief in spiritual issues (Acts 23:8). On the other hand, he frequently met the Pharisees and scribes. The reason for this was plain. All three were concerned with the moral law — Jesus with fulfilling it (Matt. 5:17) and the priests with teaching it.

A correct understanding of the law is vital, because it takes the sinner to the heart of God's righteousness and to his own need. If he is incorrect about law, he will be incorrect about holiness and grace. Thus Jesus went to the source of Israel's major problem by tackling the chief offenders. Israel's bondage was not merely political, but primarily spiritual. When the prophet Isaiah spoke of the Messiah's role of proclaiming 'liberty to the captives, and the opening of the prison to them that are bound' (Isa. 61:1), he was not referring to occupying forces, but rather to the enslavement which sin brings (John 8:34). Jesus had made this clear in one of his early sermons (Luke 4:16-20).

If only Barabbas could have understood that truth, he would not have been in the cell awaiting execution. Instead, his fury and frustrations would have been channelled in another direction, seeing the Romans in a different light. They were mere tools of Satan who was the true enemy of souls. Then might Barabbas have arrived at the same conclusions as Paul. After wringing his hands and shaking his head and crying, 'O wretched man that I am!', the apostle, who would probably have agreed with Barabbas in the early days, triumphantly answered his own question. Who could deliver him from the bondage brought about by spiritual death? 'I thank God through Jesus Christ our Lord' (Rom. 7:25).

When Pilate presented Jesus to the crowds with the words, 'Behold the man!', he unwittingly revealed more than he realized. This is the man, the only man, who can untangle the massive web which sinners have weaved. We struggle and strain to free ourselves, but to no avail. God's holy law has condemned us and guilt remains. It cannot be shaken off, only removed by Another. Jesus alone, God's only begotten Son, can enable sinners to exchange ashes, mourning and heaviness for beauty, joy and praise (Isa. 61:3).

Unlike Barabbas, Paul knew how it was accomplished: 'For what the law could not do, in that it was weak through the flesh, God sending his own Son in the likeness of sinful flesh, and for sin, condemned sin in the flesh' (Rom. 8:3). The law cannot redeem a sinner, only condemn him. This was the source of Paul's astonishing discovery. As a Pharisee, he had spent years instructing others to follow his example in trying desperately hard to live according to the standard of the law, in the hope that obedience to it might save their souls. This was the accepted teaching of the Sanhedrin, and it is the favourite doctrine of all to this day who are determined to try to redeem themselves — the doctrine of 'works'.

The law, as the reflection of God's spotless purity, is incapable of providing comfort and consolation to blemished man. His only hope lies in the one whom God sent especially for the task of making atonement for sinners. Jesus came 'in the likeness of sinful flesh' (Rom. 8:3), every inch a true man, yet completely unblemished (Heb. 4:15). He lived as every man must under the law (Gal. 4:4), and was obedient to its commands both in the letter and the spirit as no one else is. He did not slip or slide into disobedience, or cause a frown to appear upon his Father's brow, because he never failed to fulfil his will (John 6:38). Here was man as he ought to have been, and as God had always demanded he should be.

Pilate and Barabbas saw Jesus from two entirely different angles. Pilate saw only what he wanted to see: a weakened and pathetic figure. Barabbas heard only what he wanted to hear: that the miracle worker was not miraculously rescued from his own plight. The apostles, and every Christian since, share the divine view of what happened in Christ. The demands of the moral law were met, that God and one's neighbour should be loved without reserve (Matt. 22:36-40). In his Son, almighty God 'condemned sin in the flesh' (Rom. 8:3). His broken law demanded retribution, a curse upon rebellious mankind.

Through his broken body under the curse of the broken law, Jesus took the ultimate blow against sin and all uncleanness (Gal. 3:10,13). He did it for sinners, that they might have the law's righteousness fulfilled in them (Rom. 8:4) and written in their hearts (Jer. 31:31-34) and that they might be justified at the bar of heaven's justice (Ezek. 36:25-27). That is the true and only freedom, as Jesus reminded his hearers: 'If the Son therefore shall make you free, ye shall be free indeed' (John 8:36).

Yet Barabbas, who had sought so hard for freedom of a political nature, found himself behind bars chained up by the system and shackled to Satan. His had been a lost cause in every way, and in modern times when political terrorism in the desire for 'freedom' has become a way of life for many across the world, Barabbas' folly should act as a warning.

The people's choice of Barabbas

As he thought about his future, the sounds of the vast crowds not far away wafted towards him. He and his fellow prisoners guessed what was happening for not only had they heard of Jesus' arrest, but occasionally the chanting of his name could be heard reverberating around the precincts of Antonia. Soon excitement began to rise in the cells. The prisoners, with their ears pressed against the bars, could detect the sound of another name being shouted. There was no mistaking it for it was chanted in unison by hundreds: 'Barabbas!' (Matt. 27:21).

The cellmates knew what was happening, although there was more drama attached to the occasion than was normally the case. The annual custom of the governor releasing a prisoner during the passover may have proved merciful for the winner of the lottery, but for the remainder the agony was exacerbated by having been brought so close to freedom. Each prisoner must have spent the entire day up to the moment of decision in a state of extreme agitation. After all, the choice could not have been more stark: either the judicial scourging and a hideous death — or liberty. Even in that apparent act of clemency Roman cruelty was evident.

The prisoners now had no doubt who was the 'lucky' one among them; crestfallen expressions and embittered curses told their own story. The more they listened, the more confident they became that this was so. In the distance could be heard the governor's voice shouting to the vast crowds amidst the clamour, and the intermittent harshness rising up from them in a crescendo of animosity: 'Crucify him, crucify him!' (Luke 23:21).

Jesus or Barabbas! Even the villains would not have understood why the one had been chosen in preference to the other, for they would have recognized their own kind. Barabbas had faced the risks as an occupational hazard, and this time there had been one too many. Jesus, on the other hand, was decidedly different: he had not set out to make himself a hero by provoking the Romans, nor had his quarrels with the Sanhedrin deserved crucifixion. He went about doing good, without favour to any one class of people, and all the fair-minded appreciated it. He had healed and encouraged so many during his years of ministry, hardly a family in the land could have been left untouched by his influence (Matt. 4:23-25).

Why, then, had Barabbas been chosen? The prisoners surely discussed the question among themselves, not as a merely academic pursuit, for their lives had quite literally depended upon the decision Pilate had just made at the insistence of the mob. Why had he not chosen one of them? At best they would spend years suffering behind bars, at worst hours or even days hanging on a cross until dead. For their own satisfaction they had to find an answer.

Barabbas knew what it was. Robber and murderer he may have been, but he was not insignificant. Having sought to wring the Roman eagle's neck with his small band of patriots, he had become a peg upon which the national aspirations were hung. Barabbas was the focal point for any discussion regarding the future of Israel, and as such his concept of freedom was the one which reflected the nation's mood.

That mood was dismal, filled with unrequited hope. Since the days beyond the Exile, almost 600 years earlier, when God revealed truth to the prophets and the Messianic hope rose high in Israel's consciousness, there had been a steady decline in the people's anticipation. True, in Babylon great men like Ezekiel and Daniel had kept the prophetic fire ablaze, but once the Jews returned to their homeland after seventy years the flame slowly became a flicker (Jer. 25:11). What belief remained in a 'Messianic hope' was added to the confusing plethora of ideas on the subject.

For at least 400 years Israel had been living among the ashes of a deepening despair. Like that of Gideon in a former age, Israel's mood was reflected in a series of rhetorical questions: 'Oh my Lord, if the Lord be with us, why ...?' (Judg. 6:13). No doubt during those four centuries (the inter-testamental period) was heard the psalmist's prayer: 'We have heard with our ears, O God, our fathers have told us, what work thou didst in their days, in the times of old' (Ps. 44:1).

With the sudden arrival of John the Baptist the dying embers were rekindled. For months, hope warmed the hearts of multitudes as they gathered at the Jordan river to have their wilting faith strengthened by the fiery prophet of Judæa. The smallest corner of Israel could not have avoided the excitement engendered by the powerful and appealing messages delivered by this unusual messenger from God. He was 'Elijah' promised to Israel (Matt. 17:10-13), appointed to prepare the Messiah's way (Mal. 4:5-6). Jesus carried the torch still further. Israel had not witnessed its equal before, and it lasted for several years.

The national enthusiasm knew no bounds, apart from the scepticism and opposition of the Sanhedrin, but this only served to heighten the electrifying awareness that the Messiah had truly arrived to usher in a new age in which Israel would be vindicated and foreign powers condemned. God had heard their cries and sighs, as he had during the days of Egyptian bondage (Exod. 2:23-25), and had come to rescue them!

But with John's execution, and later Jesus' arrest, the nation experienced an anticlimax, as reflected in the despondency of the men on the Emmaus road (Luke 24:19-21). All the old frustrations returned with increasing anguish, the national mood was bitter, and it was not difficult to blame Jesus of Nazareth. The people, having sought to make him a king (John 6:15), had harnessed their hopes to him, and in return, he had smashed their dreams! The line between adulation and disillusionment is at times paper-thin.

It would not have been too difficult in the circumstances, therefore, for the Sanhedrin to encourage the people to choose Barabbas in preference to Jesus. The disappointment had rapidly turned into an appreciation of Barabbas' courage in the face of the enemy, and recognition of his ideals. In the heat of the debate even his villainy was overlooked. He had at least attempted to free his people, and not just talked about it! (John 8:32,36).

Freedom — true and false

On trial before Pilate, and the world, were not only two prisoners representing good and evil, but two concepts about freedom. The issue is just as relevant today. What can affect the greater change for the better in society — the preaching of the crucified, risen and ascended Christ, or the use of weaponry? Should mankind hasten to the prayer closet, or to the armoury? In other words, does society require a revival or a revolution? On the original 'Good Friday', the decision was taken. Barabbas was hailed as the Jewish reply to the nation's oppression, that is, to employ all the physical means at the state's disposal and without reference to almighty God. Terrorism today agrees (2 Cor. 10:4).

Guards sent at the command of the governor marched towards the cells. Barabbas, with probably a wink and a jeer at his fellow prisoners, was set free. It was the 'luckiest' day of his life. He had expected and deserved death, but instead Jesus, his substitute, had secured the sinner's freedom. He would not have appreciated it, for the irony would have eluded him, but Barabbas had particpated in a gospel parable.

Still, he was free — or was he? Had this not been the fundamental argument discussed throughout the land during Jesus' ministry? What is freedom? The governor had opened the prison doors to set Barabbas free, but only the Saviour could have erased the sins which had imprisoned him. He had been freed by the Roman court, but not at the bar of divine justice, where to be justified in the sight of God is the true and ultimate freedom (Rom. 5:1).

Barabbas left Antonia and disappeared into the mists of history. What became of him is unknown. It seems likely he was like the proverbial dog who 'turned to his own vomit again' (2 Peter 2:22), preferring the choice of the natural man, 'darkness rather than light', because of his evil deeds (John 3:19). Pilate, on the other hand, brought to the edge of truth by Truth himself, finally rejected it. Cæsar's pomp and power, already fading, proved more tangible than any unseen kingdom Jesus knew (2 Cor. 4:18). The governor's loyalty to the temporal powers was not rewarded, however. Not long after the events of that morning he was sacked, ending his days in Gaul where he eventually committed suicide.

For both men it is an eternal irony that they were to meet the man from Galilee again (John 5:22-29), wearing a crown and majestic robe and with a sceptre in his hand (Rev. 19:11-16), but this time he would be seated! (2 Cor. 5:10). In the meantime the sinner's only hope was led away, the 'scapegoat' taken into the wilderness to suffer a lonely death bearing the sins of the people (Lev. 16:20-22) — to die as a common villain (Isa. 53:6).

8.
Ascent to Skull Hill

By this time, the two thieves who had shared with Barabbas the emotional agony experienced in the cells were brought to join Jesus. Nervous tension, the immense strain of the occasion and above all the judicial scourging would have meant that all three showed signs of acute exhaustion. Haggard and hollow-eyed, with sweat covering their faces and blood trickling down their backs, there still lay ahead of them the nightmare trudge to Skull Hill and the actual crucifixions.

The spectators of this pitiful sight must have wondered whether Jesus and his companions would be capable of proceeding, but the Roman centurion had other ideas. The custom dictated that each condemned prisoner should carry the crossbeam to Calvary, and as the beam had to support the full weight of a dying man it was an extremely heavy piece of thick tree-trunk. Without consideration for the victim, muscular arms and the rough hands of Roman legionaries tied the beam to outstretched arms with twine. The splintered wood rubbed repeatedly with each painful movement upon an already chafed neck and shoulders. Weakened legs buckled under the weight.

The procession set off very slowly, consisting of a motley array of unlikely companions: Jesus, two thieves, a centurion and four legionaries (John 19:23). The three at the centre swayed and stumbled, borne on by the momentum of the crossbeams, each one dictating the direction its carrier would go. At times Jesus fell and surely the thieves did too, and without arms free to cushion the impact, their faces hit the rocky ground with full force. Grazed and bruised, with fresh blood oozing from noses, they were urged on with harsh commands and the vigorous use of the centurion's cane. It was important to keep the procession moving, difficult though it was proving to be.

This was so because of the numbers of excited and inquisitive spectators who had gathered to watch the proceedings. It is an aspect of man's fallen nature that he feels the need to gape at the misfortunes of others. They surged forward, their necks straining for a closer glimpse, the legionaries seeking to contain their eagerness by roughly pushing them back. Then there was the noise: jeering men, screaming women, shouted commands, the swish of the cane, the whine of the whips and the grunts and groans of men in pain — this was the backcloth to Jesus' approach to Skull Hill.

Mixed attitudes in the crowd

Not all the spectators of his solemn journey shared in the general ferocity. Scattered throughout the jostling crowds were many who were sympathetic for one reason or another: for example, the disciples who had shared an early passover meal with him the previous evening. Their feelings are best imagined; having deserted him at the moment he needed them most, they must have remained on the periphery of the crowds fearful of showing their faces (Matt. 26:56). They knew it was too late to do anything about their Master's predicament, and would have blamed themselves for it.

Others shared a genuine admiration for Jesus, even if they were unable to understand the teaching or fathom the significance of his ministry. They just wanted to be with him, especially when he had made his way to Jerusalem for the final time (Luke 9:51). There had been occasions when their zeal to be in the company of so famous a figure (whom they had once sought to make their king, John 6:15) far outweighed any commitment they thought they possessed for his cause (Luke 9:57-62).

For these people mere sentiment played a large part in their attraction to him, an unreliable refuge sought by those devoid of eternal truth. It manifested itself by replacing admiration for Jesus with devotion for his mother, a notion which found no sympathy with him. 'Blessed is the womb that bare thee', one such lady exclaimed, to which Jesus retorted, 'Yea, rather, blessed are they that hear the word of God, and keep it' (Luke 11:27,28). Again, sentiment was expressed by those who were prepared to accept the sweeter aspects of his ministry whilst rejecting that which clashed with their preconceived ideas. Jesus lost many followers from among such people (John 6:60-66).

There was no doubt that the crowd which gathered that eventful morning mirrored the whole range of prevailing views about Jesus of Nazareth, from outright hatred to deep thankfulness. There were many who loathed him, for he had revealed their hypocrisy too often, either with the penetrating glance of perfect holiness (Luke 22:61), or with the sternness of the spoken word (Matt. 23). His spotless purity, for which there could be no hint of affectation, instinctively lit up the shadowy corners of others' lives. He did not search for sin: there was no need; his silent presence was sufficient for it to creep from its hiding-place. He is the Light in a very dark world (John 12:46).

But that light not only exposed sin and uncleanness; it bathed the needy in the warmth of his generous compassion. The downcast, outcast, the deprived and demented — all held his attention, received his love, felt his touch. Jesus had sat at the lowliest of hearths, had heard the faintest of heart-cries, held the frailest of hands, strengthened the weakest of the weak, knelt at the bedside of the aged and lovingly whispered his gospel into the ears of the dying.

Throughout Israel, and in regions beyond the Jordan, scarcely a family had been left untouched by the gracious provision of his powers (Matt. 4:23-24). Impossibility had been conquered, hopelessness erased: sight given to the blind, hearing to the deaf, ability to the disabled — even the dead had been raised. Nobody could have disputed it (Acts 10:38). Numerous were the prayers of thanksgiving for Jesus of Nazareth.

Simon the Cyrenian

The procession stopped again. Each time it did so, the onlookers by strength of numbers came close to engulfing the pathetic figures on their way to Calvary. There was no alternative: progress had ground to a halt as Jesus sank to his knees once more. Patience was probably not a centurion's strong point, and after applying his cane to the prisoner as he would have done to a mule, he decided there was only one thing to do. Glancing hastily around he caught sight of a strong young man being swept along in the crush. At a signal to one of his legionaries, the inquisitive spectator was hastily pulled from the sidelines and ordered to bear Jesus' heavy load (Mark 15:21).

He was Simon, who had travelled to Jerusalem with his family from Cyrene — Tripoli in Libya — to celebrate the passover. The Jewish community to which they belonged was a large one, made famous because of its stand against the Romans during the Maccabæan period nearly two centuries earlier. As a consequence, the Cyrenian Jews gained an influence far from home; in fact they were prominent in Jerusalem itself and bitterly opposed to Jesus' followers (Acts 6:9).

What the feelings of the young man were as he picked up the unwanted burden are not known, but an intelligent guess can be made. He might have mused on how quickly circumstances can change — one moment a mere spectator of the ghastly scene and the next a central part of it! Besides, for how long would he be caught up in all this? His family would wonder where he was. He, a proud Cyrenian Jew assisting the Romans! Worse, and the irony of the situation would not have escaped him, here he was walking beside Jesus and assisting him, yet he was numbered among those who hated him.

Like Barabbas, Simon was also unwittingly involved in a gospel parable. That morning he would have taken his paschal lamb to the temple as was expected of him, and joined hundreds of others in the Levitical rites performed there on such occasions (Lev. 1). Later in the day he would collect the carcase, the blood having been drained away in the temple precincts, so that his wife could treat it in readiness for the passover meal in the evening (Exod. 12:1-10). Now he found himself, perhaps with the blood of the sacrificial lamb still on his hands, the companion of the paschal Lamb of God on his way to the sacrifice (John 1:29,36).

Again, had Simon not been drawn 'irresistibly' to Jesus (Mark 15:21), and was he not obliged to carry his cross as the Lord demands of all his disciples? (Luke 14:27). Furthermore, being identified with the Son of God, he could no longer remain a spectator. He was now in the thick of it with the Saviour, and there was no possibility of escape. Or as the New Testament reminds us, 'Jesus also, that he might sanctify the people with his own blood, suffered without the gate. Let us go forth therefore unto him without the camp, bearing his reproach' (Heb. 13:12-13). The painful lashes, the howls of the mob and the gesticulating arms of abuse were now an unwelcome feature of Simon's life as well as that of Jesus. He was 'one' with the Lord (Gal. 2:20).

The wailing women

Amid the tumult as the procession made its tortuous way towards the city gate in sight of Calvary, the sounds of wailing could be distinctly heard. A group of local women, remaining as close to Jesus as possible despite difficulties, kept up a continuous lamentation such as is typical in the Orient (Luke 23:27-28). They were not only weeping, but giving vent to an excessive emotional vigour typical of the professional mourners of that period (Luke 8:52). It was probably their custom to attend all such tragic occasions as men were led to their deaths, in which case they performed their duties well, for their wailing continued almost unabated throughout the proceedings. Against the background of curses, lashes and alarm the sounds of the sobbing women could not have instilled much comfort into the three victims.

It may have been as the procession was about to pass through the city gate, beyond which few spectators would normally have been allowed to draw near, that Jesus had an opportunity to preach his final sermon, which would have been overheard and noted by

Simon. The intensity with which Jesus spoke to the women under such circumstances, together with the solemn content of his message, caused them to cease their ostentatious display: 'Daughters of Jerusalem, weep not for me, but weep for yourselves, and for your children' (Luke 23:28). So unexpected was the sudden outburst, the words flew like arrows from the bow.

The women had seen men in this terrible situation before, exhaustion and physical agony forbidding any conversation other than groans and oaths uttered through swollen lips. Thus when a man approaching death and facing the horrors of crucifixion summoned up the necessary strength to make a final appeal he had to be listened to. In fact, as far as we know, those words were the only ones Jesus spoke on the way to Golgotha. Simon, who was near at hand, heard them — words which helped change his life.

It came as a surprise to the women to have their tearful sympathy overruled by Jesus' challenge. A wretched prisoner on the way to an execution was hardly in a position to refuse their sympathy. He even went so far as to say that they should weep for themselves! Jesus was not impatient, as others might have been in the circumstances, but compassionate, although he considered their wailing irrelevant.

It surely was obvious to the women that he genuinely cared about their welfare, although whether they ever came to appreciate why this was so is not known. Unlike the Galilean women who followed Jesus to the south for the passover (Luke 23:49), the 'daughters of Jerusalem' were not believers in the gospel Jesus had preached throughout the land. Their emotions were dancing on their sleeves, and as they were in need of an understanding of God's ways, their motives required examination. It is tragically possible to believe in the validity of one's actions, yet fail to realize that God disowns them. As he once declared to Isaiah, 'My thoughts are not your thoughts, neither are your ways my ways... For as the heavens are higher than the earth, so are my ways higher than your ways, and my thoughts than your thoughts' (Isa. 55:8-9). How careful we need to be!

In regarding the women's action as irrelevant, Jesus was not belittling the tears of the genuinely sorrowful. Far from it! The shortest verse in the Scriptures ('Jesus wept') reveals the tenderness of his heart towards human suffering (John 11:35). Had he not wept on the Mount of Olives while considering Jerusalem's plight? (Luke 19:41). His tears, though, were never shed for superficial or sentimental reasons, but from the depth of spiritual concern. When he stood before the tomb of his friend Lazarus, he witnessed the sorrow all around him from a confused and unbelieving people. They recognized Jesus' power to give sight to the blind, even his ability to preserve the sick from death (John 11:37), but failed to believe in his authority over death itself. Once Lazarus died the mourners abandoned all hope.

Even his friend Martha chided him with the hurtful suggestion that had Jesus been present, her brother would not have died. She believed her Lord could heal from near at hand, but not from afar, and even less that he could actually raise the dead! (John 11:21). Jesus wept. The Prince of life was in their midst (Acts 3:15), and despite all his remarkable miracles his friends still believed in the power of death. How many believers in modern times have this problem, and possess a faith stronger in theory than in practice!

As for these 'daughters' of Jerusalem, how grieving it must have been for Jesus to hear the unconverted weeping on his behalf, however sincerely! In expressing sorrow for Jesus they were completely unconcerned about their own situation. His eventual destination was glory, but unless they repented, theirs was everlasting condemnation. Yet they wept for *him*! How tragic that they were unaware that shortly afterwards he would be seated majestically at the right hand of God! (Heb. 12:2). The world is never in a position to pity the followers of Jesus; they are in possession of too many privileges and benefits. It is the world which requires compassion.

No doubt there were many in Jerusalem that morning who shared the views expressed by the wailing women, and certainly there have been many more since then. They watched Jesus making his way to Calvary, a young man who had done so much good (Acts 10:38), and considered it all a dreadful mistake. Even the Roman governor, who was far removed from any spiritual understanding, was forced to admit that he found 'no cause of death in him'. So why was he about to be killed? (Luke 23:22). Those holding such views recognize Jesus' goodness, and may even be prepared to admit they believe he was the greatest of all human beings, but they refuse to go further. To them he ended his days tragically, a martyr dying for a good cause, and if only his example would be followed by everyone what a better place the world would be!

In other words, they emphasize Jesus' living rather than his dying, his character and not his cross. After a life of such purity and promise the excruciating agonies of a crucifixion seemed cruel, and unnecessary, for a virile young man of thirty-three or so to be forced to endure. The women saw the weals of the whips across his back and winced with pity when he staggered and fell to the ground, only to be kicked into action each time. They thought, as women would, of their husbands, sons and brothers in a similar situation.

There was no sympathy offered to Jesus' two companions in tribulation, for their wickedness was undeserving of it, but the distress and death of so noble a character as that of Jesus seemed such a waste. The futility of it called for lamentation. Sadly it illustrates that even when people are involved in worship at one of the most important feasts of the year, spiritual blindness will dictate what is understood, and rob the individual of God's smile.

The unregenerate are incapable of appreciating the dire consequences of their sin, the 'wages' of which are 'death' (Rom. 6:23), and therefore the dangers they face from the righteous anger of almighty God. If he is 'angry with the wicked every day', can the unregenerate expect much less? (Ps. 7:11). Yet they continue along life's pathway unable to see the precipice ahead. They may express an admiration for Jesus, may even weep for him and consider his teaching important but, like the wailing women of Jerusalem, they resemble those who are without sight, or even eyes. As Toplady put it in his famous hymn,

> Not the labours of my hands
> Can fulfil thy law's demands;
> Could my zeal no respite know,
> Could my tears for ever flow,
> All for sin could not atone,
> Thou must save, and thou alone.

The destruction of Jerusalem foretold

If the women were ignorant of living under the threat of God's wrath, there was another danger they faced which was more readily understood and was shared by the nation as a whole. They must have been struck, as was Simon, by the urgency in Jesus' voice: 'For, behold, the days are coming, in the which they shall say, Blessed are the barren, and the wombs that never bare, and the paps which never gave suck. Then shall they begin to say to the mountains, Fall on us; and to the hills, Cover us' (Luke 23:29-30). It is typical of those in need of spiritual enlightenment that although they are unable to fear the prospect of *everlasting* condemnation, they tremble at the mention of a *temporary* catastrophe.

Jesus anticipated, and had already wept over, a holocaust worse than any other in Israel's turbulent history up till then (Luke 19:41-44). The suicide of one individual is a tragedy but 'they' — multitudes within the Jewish nation — would seek 'comfort' in being engulfed by mountains rather than have to endure the impending disaster. Had Simon and the women been familiar with the prophetic writings, they would have remembered that an almost identical expression (although with a fascinating difference) was used by God when addressing Hosea to warn him of Samaria's downfall in 721B.C. (see Hosea 10:8).

Now it was to be Jerusalem's turn. The prophecy was that the people experiencing the divine displeasure would seek the same violent end to their lives, and for the same reasons. If Israel was 'bent to backsliding' from God (Hosea 11:7), who from an immense love had secured her rescue from Egypt, what retribution could be expected for Israel's condemnation and crucifixion of his Son? If such 'fires' were lit when Judaism's 'tree' was moist-green (Luke 23:31), one should be horrified to contemplate what was going to occur when it was tinder dry (see Epilogue).

Arrival at Calvary

The place of execution was feared by the people, with everyone keeping a safe distance from the area under normal circumstances

— but this was not a normal day. Jesus of Nazareth was being executed. The wailing women would probably have ceased their ritual and returned home, another morning's work completed. Simon, though, was obliged to continue. Through the city gate he and his three companions trudged, leaving behind them Jerusalem's familiar sights and sounds. They were now not far from their destination.

The heat of a new day had already made its presence felt, the blazing sun, nearing its zenith in a cloudless sky, pounding the men remorselessly. Sweat saturated their bodies, the dusty pathway bathed them in grime and the burdens grew heavier with each faltering step they took. The centurion and his men did not escape the pressure, with helmets and breastplates generating more heat than comfort. Simon must have wondered what his family would think if they could see him, and in any case they would by now have been anxious about his failure to return to them.

The overpowering noise of the mob had given way to quieter sounds, the heavy breathing of exhausted men occasionally collapsing on to the hard ground and the accompanying swish of a lash, but the terror increased as the destination drew closer. It was no place for the faint-hearted. Simon knew his aching muscles would soon be relieved, that he would be permitted to hurry away, but what of those he would leave behind? He had experienced a little of their sufferings, although not a scourging, but what lay ahead for them would be much worse. Men had been known to hang upon crosses in all weathers, crying out in agony, for hours, or even days, before death seized them. Simon shuddered.

One thing he knew: he could never be the same man again. It was not only the earnest message he had heard, although that had alarmed him, but the person himself who had enthralled him. He still has the same effect on people today. Accompanying Jesus of Nazareth, the one he later realized was the Messiah, to Calvary had radically changed Simon. From a few feet away, he had been able to observe Jesus closely against an ungodly background of clamour, curses, indignity, abuse and pain. How much easier had it been for him to teach his disciples on the gentle slopes overlooking the shimmering waters of Galilee's lake (Matt. 5-7), but now those lessons had to be put into practice. They were. The gracious humility, the silent forbearance, the tender concern for others and even the expression of love for his enemies — these qualities did not belong in such an environment, except to one who was divinely unique.

They had arrived. For a criminal condemned to die by crucifixion on the mound, the first sight of Calvary was undoubtedly terrifying. Even the most hardened of villains would have wanted to run from the place, anywhere, to escape from what was about to take place. It was impossible. A sense of finality hung over Golgotha, aptly called 'a place of a skull' (Matt. 27:33), more akin to the dead than the living. It was a bleak and barren spot. Once having reached it the doomed never returned. If only it was all a dream, a nightmare, and one was about to awaken to reality! But to the victims Skull Hill, and what it contained, was the only reality left to them.

Simon's work over, he was free to return to his family, with surely a backward glance at the one he had assisted, and is it possible to imagine him not receiving a smile in return? The morning had proved momentous, the turning-point in his life. In the months ahead he was drawn to Christ again, this time by the Holy Spirit, in a union which was to last for ever. His wife and sons joined him among the ranks of the redeemed (Mark 15:21) and, having to leave the Jewish community in Cyrene where their new-found Lord was hated, they settled in Rome. There eventually they became prominent members of the church and were befriended by the apostle Paul (Rom. 16:13).

The crucifixion

In the meantime, as Simon breathed a sigh of relief that his fearful journey had ended, his three former companions ascended the mound and then slumped to the ground beyond their tether. They could do no more; submission to the inevitable was all that was left. Nearby lay a leather pouch of nails, a hammer or two, some twine and three sturdy tree-trunks: not much, but sufficient to send shivers up the spine!

Soon the only sounds that could be heard were those of hammering, each dull thud a reminder of the dreadful occasion, as the crossbeams were placed into position. It was a difficult task and had to be done efficiently, the crosses having to support the weight of dying men. It is left to the imagination to visualize what thoughts would pass through a condemned man's mind at that moment, but one can be confident of knowing where Jesus' thoughts lay. It was for that 'hour' he had been born (John 12:27). It was a time for prayer.

It was never straightforward crucifying a man. By this time probably too weak to stand, he was dragged by the soldiers to the assembled cross lying on the ground. Struggling was pointless. His arms were then tightly bound to the beams with the twine, his legs to the base of the tree, and when this task was completed the legionaries lifted the cross and with great effort managed to slot it into the hole in the ground already dug for it.

It was at that moment the excruciating pain began. Already the twine binding his naked arms and legs had affected the circulation and cramp had set it, but when the cross dropped into the slot in the ground the twine tightened, cutting into the flesh and the man's entire body jolted. His arms, which supported his full weight, were now out of joint and the rib-cage shifted its position, making it harder for him to breathe. From then on there could be no respite from the agony, which increased as the minutes ticked away.

It appears the two thieves were crucified first, because when it was Jesus' turn there was a sudden change of plan. It was decided, perhaps at the suggestion of the authorities who feared the possibility of his escape even at so late an hour, that Jesus' suffering should be more acute. Accompanying the binding with twine, large nails would secure his hands and feet. The leather pouch was called for, but the officer and his legionaries were unaware they were fulfilling Scripture prophecy: 'They pierced my hands and my feet' (Ps. 22:16).

Another reason for believing that Jesus was left to the last was that crucifying him would have taken much longer to carry out. Perhaps two of the soldiers worked together, securing a hand each, but the penetration of flesh by an iron nail would not have been a simple undertaking. It took a number of heavy blows, each one producing agonized cries, before the numbed hands were pinioned to the wood. It was then the turn of the feet.

Jesus' body shook and trembled as shock waves affected the central nervous system, and muscular spasms set in. It would not have been surprising had he fainted. The expected jolt when the cross shuddered into position caused the nails to tear angrily at the flesh, a situation which could only get worse. The psalmist painted the gruesome picture with a few deft strokes when he heard the Messiah crying out, 'All my bones are out of joint... I may tell all my bones' (Ps. 22:14,17).

Despite this, when he was offered sour wine 'mingled with gall' (as we assume the thieves also were) to dull the pain, Jesus, having tasted the fluid, refused to drink (Matt. 27:34). He knew his 'cup of suffering' endured for sinners had to be drunk to the dregs; the bitterness of its taste could not be mellowed artificially, any more than their sin can be 'sanitized' in God's sight. Man's fall, in *total*, is answered for sinners by Christ's offer of salvation in *full*.

The onlookers

The crosses erected to the centurion's satisfaction, with Jesus occupying the central position (Matt. 27:38), Calvary was suddenly no longer the lonely spot it had been. No doubt to the soldiers' surprise, groups of visitors appeared from various directions — an unusual occurrence (Luke 23:48). The presence of so many would not have been welcomed by the Roman authorities, who would have feared the possibility of trouble, but as leading members of the Sanhedrin were among them it was probably thought best to ignore the intrusion.

The priests came from the direction of Jerusalem and were accompanied by a group of hangers-on, who had taken advantage of the Sanhedrin's presence to give vent to their feelings. In fact, as their taunts echoed the erroneous statements of the false witnesses made the night before and known only to those present at Jesus' 'trial', they had probably been invited along by the priests to add to the Sanhedrin's abusiveness (Matt. 26:60-61).

Unlike the priests they did not remain, but before leaving they enjoyed themselves at Jesus' expense, and in doing so revealed their own inadequacies (Matt. 27:39-40). In a way typical of their kind, they expressed their opposition from the comparative safety of the group, gaining strength in numbers and encouraging each other in their callous behaviour. These were the 'swine' before whom the gospel should not be cast (Matt. 7:6), so brutish and insensitive to heaven's overshadowing that they trampled upon the precious 'pearls' of revealed truth with impunity.

Not content with that, in hating the message they trampled upon the Messenger also, despite his appalling suffering. This 'Son of God' believed that single-handed he could pull down Jerusalem's mighty temple, and then restore it in a mere three days, when it had already taken the workmen forty-six years to build — and they still had not finished it! It would have been easier for him to descend from the cross. They left Skull Hill assuming they had seen the last of Jesus of Nazareth (John 2:18-21).

By this time many others had arrived in the vicinity, some because their love for Jesus would not let them stay away (Matt. 27:55-56). They had to express their sympathy, albeit from a distance, in the only way they knew (Luke 23:49). However, most managed to get as close as possible to the gruesome scene to satisfy their curiosity. It is doubtful whether the soldiers had ever seen so many spectators at Calvary.

The priests' hatred of Jesus

The contemptuous tirade sparked off a chain reaction (Matt. 27:39-44). Soon the air was filled with abuse and blasphemy as, not for the first time (John 8:59), the religious leaders shamelessly laid aside the dignity of their office and behaved in a manner which must have shocked even the pagan Romans at the scene. It revealed how far the priesthood had wandered from its divine origins, when Aaron's sons were especially anointed for service and their priestly garments were 'for glory and for beauty' (Exod. 28:40).

Little attempt was made to control themselves as their seething hatred for Jesus, which had spilled over violently the night before (Matt. 26:67), continued to express itself. It might be thought that everything had already been said, but there was much more vicious-ness to gush from them, in a plethora of vindictive remarks. Nailed to the cross, with his life slowly and agonizingly ebbing away, Jesus was a captive audience in more ways than one. He was cornered.

The priests, though, were cunning. Unlike the scoffing passers-by, who aimed their verbal darts directly at Jesus (Matt. 27:40), the black-robed accusers did not. Although their anger was hurled at him, their words were for other ears also: '*He* saved others... If *he* be the King of Israel... *He* trusted in God... *He* said, I am the Son of God...' (Matt. 27:42-43). In other words, the members of the Sanhedrin had taken the trouble to visit Skull Hill to watch Jesus die, not only to mock him, but to vindicate their own position in the eyes of all the citizens of Jerusalem, if not of Israel itself. They believed the onlookers would spread their message.

From their 'pulpit' on the mound within a short distance of Jesus, whose twisted form illustrated something of his physical torment, the priests launched into a fiery attack upon him: 'Look at him — so much for his claims! Is this pathetic individual the King of Israel, the Son of God and Saviour of sinners? If he is, now is the time to prove it.' All he had to do to convince the onlookers, Israel and indeed the world, was to escape from his tragic dilemma and miraculously descend from the cross. But even as they spoke, those with an atom of scriptural understanding who listened to the tirade would have realized they had heard those mocking words before (Matt. 27:43). Across the millennium which separated the psalmist from the Sanhedrin came the familiar challenge: 'He trusted on the Lord that he would deliver him: let him deliver him, seeing he delighted in him' (Ps. 22:8). Heaven appeared to be deriding their efforts.

It was a blasphemous harangue, by which the Sanhedrin was telling the nation, 'We told you so.' Throughout the previous three years the council's authority had been greatly eroded — an authority which had its origins deep within Jewish history (Num. 11:16-30) — as a result of an astonishing phenomenon which had arisen in Israel and which was mentioned in the previous chapter. A religious awakening had stirred the land and also the neighbouring territories (Matt. 4:24-25), when the mighty preaching of John the Baptist captivated vast crowds with fascinating sermons informing everyone the Messiah had arrived (Luke 3:1-18). Shortly afterwards his cousin Jesus, a Galilean young man of thirty years (Luke 3:23), entered Judea and took control of the movement. The members of the council were deeply disturbed by what had happened, but worse was to follow (John 1:19-28).

News reached them from the north, so alarming they could hardly believe it, about the controversial preaching of this carpenter. He had been thrust out of Nazareth's synagogue when quoting from the book of Isaiah (61:1-3), because he had implied that he was the Messiah spoken about by the prophet (Luke 4:16-30). Worse still, they had heard his followers were astonished when he presumed to give them the definitive meaning of God's holy law. (Rabbinical teaching emphasized only its letter, but Jesus had taken the disciples right to its heart, revealing the spirit of the law.) The Almighty had written it on tablets of stone with his own finger (Exod. 31:18), yet this young man when referring to the law audaciously stated, 'But I say unto you...'! (Matt. 5). What else was he suggesting, but that he was no less than equal with God himself? (John 5:18).

From that moment there was no holding the crowds back. They believed Jesus' authority to be divine (Matt. 7:28-29), and therefore that it superseded that of the rabbis, who they insisted were envious of him (Matt. 27:18). He had even established what appeared to them as his own 'sanhedrin'! (Luke 10:1). At one stage the people had thought of making him their king, but he had no intention of complying with their wishes (John 6:15). The miraculous events, the vigorous debates with council members and the awesome displays of anger when daring to clear out the temple (on two occasions) — this had been the situation for three long years, culminating in his triumphant entry into Jerusalem accompanied by thousands of jubilant supporters shouting victoriously 'Hosanna to the son of David, Blessed is he that cometh in the name of the Lord; Hosanna in the highest' (Matt. 21:9).

Well, now look at him — a crumpled figure on a Roman gibbet, deity unable to help itself! How could anyone be envious of Jesus? He was finished, his cause lost! The 'sermon' had proved effective, the priests satisfied, as others at the site took up the cudgels. The two villains (Matt. 27:44) and the Roman soldiers, whose ignorance of the issues was plain to see, nevertheless mocked Jesus about matters of which they knew nothing (Luke 23:36-37).

Desolation and darkness

To those present who loved the Saviour, especially his mother standing with her friends at the foot of the cross (John 19:25), it was a depressing and lonely moment. Golgotha was always a friendless place, but now much more so. The blessed times seemed over, stripped away with only faith remaining. Anticlimax substituted for hope had set in (Luke 24:19-21). Satan was taunting, asking where was their God and the ungodly were triumphing over them (Ps. 42:10).

Where indeed was God? It was a question for which Jesus' two companions demanded an answer and, not receiving satisfaction, they turned on him. They were desperate. If Jesus claimed to be God's Son, why did he not rescue the three of them from this appalling situation? They expected the miraculous, but all they got were prayers! They looked out from their crosses and cursed; he looked upwards to heaven and blessed. What a bitter disappointment he was, and they told him so in no uncertain terms (Luke 23:34,39).

Occasionally, the soldiers offered Jesus sour wine to wet his parched lips, but did so mockingly. Cruelty was second nature to them, not least when they sorted out the clothing of their prisoners among themselves. It was one of the perks of the job. While the naked victims groaned in agony a mere glance away, the legionaries obscenely chose from their belongings the items they intended taking back to barracks with them. The gesture served to underline to the tragic and suffering men the pathos behind their situation, that they were now considered of less use than bits of cloth.

Jesus' clothing was of particular interest to them, souvenirs of their time stationed abroad to show their families in Rome. What a great deal they had to tell them! His robe held a fascination for them, or rather its hem, as from what they had heard it possessed magical qualities. By merely touching it people were healed (Luke 8:43-44). The four soldiers knew nothing about faith. They squatted on the parched earth nearby deciding what to do with this seamless outer garment, too precious to tear, and agreed to dice for it (John 19:23). They had no idea their action was being observed from above, that history knew of it or that the owner, being familiar with the Scriptures, had in any case anticipated what they would do (Ps. 22:18).

Three hours had crept by since the traumatic events at Calvary had begun that morning, and noon was usually the hottest time of the day, but not that Friday. The commotion had been such, the attention upon Jesus so concentrated, that nobody had noticed that nature desired to reflect the mood. A gentle breeze wafted across the hill, flecks of rain accompanying it, and grey clouds appeared as if from nowhere and glided past the sun creating shadows across the landscape (Ps. 18:9).

With the swiftness for which changes in weather patterns are noted in Israel, the giant hand of a sovereign God drew a black blanket across the entire country (Matt. 27:45). The crowds at Golgotha stared skywards in disbelief; people throughout the land rushed around in fear wondering what it all meant; torches were hastily lit in every home. The Creator and Sustainer of all things hung limply, dying (Col. 1:15-17), and he made the darkness his 'secret place' from the eyes of the ungodly (Ps. 18:11). Nature responded, withdrawing its charms; cattle ceased from grazing, birds from singing. How could they do otherwise on such a day?

Suddenly, from the angry clouds gushed rain which flowed in torrents from Skull Hill. The plateau quickly became a quagmire, through which the priests lifting their robes slithered from the scene as swiftly as they could, their sandals more suitable for terra firma. Observing them scurrying in all directions Jesus would have remembered the psalmist's encouraging words: 'Let God arise, let his enemies be scattered: let them also that hate him flee before him' (Ps. 68:1). The priests were not alone in leaving the area as quickly as possible. It appears likely that only the figures on the cross, the soldiers, John, Mary and her companions remained. One could not imagine a mother leaving her son at such a time, despite the horror of the occasion.

Penetrating the clouds were flashes of lightning, dazzling arrows shot from God's powerful arms, which momentarily spotlighted the crosses and the writhing figures hanging on them. Hailstones peppered their naked bodies, from which blood, sweat and rain dripped freely, and the tightened twine bit still deeper into weakened flesh. Cries were shouted to the skies as 'the Highest gave his voice' (Ps. 18:12-15).

With thunder rolling above his head, the earth rumbling beneath his feet and the winds howling all around him, the centurion shouted commands to his men they had difficulty in hearing. They had experienced hard-fought battles with enemies they could see, but what chance did Roman power have against the unseen God, especially when he rode upon 'the wings of the wind'? (Ps. 18:10). As expected he won the war, the centurion (and perhaps his men, Luke 23:34) believing in Christ before the end of that dreadful day (Matt. 27:54).

They had practical problems too. The crosses, weighted with their dying occupants, were in danger of falling. The mud had loosened its grip upon them and the winds, blowing fiercely, caused them to sway. The twine tightened still further around numbed and swollen arms and legs, the nails in Jesus' body pulling violently against his flesh. There were three crosses, but only five soldiers! The guards, never daring to forsake their duties, slithered from one to another endeavouring to keep them in position, their sandals no match for the slippery surface beneath them. Crucifixions were plentiful, but never had there been one like this before.

For three hours, from noon until mid-afternoon (Matt. 27:45), lighted torches flickered throughout the land as the people tried to come to terms with the phenomenon. Everyone trembled, but those knowledgeable in scriptural matters more so, believing the experience to be apocalyptic. They would have remembered Joel's prophetic words: 'And I will show wonders in the heavens and in the earth, blood, and fire, and pillars of smoke. The sun shall be turned into darkness, and the moon into blood, before the great and terrible day of the Lord come' (Joel 2:30-31). They must have thought the end had arrived, when in fact the glorious beginning was within reach (Acts 2:14-24).

The two thieves

If the entire country felt the impact of the divine displeasure, for the Father made sure nobody would be indifferent to his Son's atoning sacrifice, the focal point was the plateau of Skull Hill. There the elements were unleashed with particular fury, the three crosses shuddering and swaying in the driving, breathtaking winds and rain, the drenched figures on them intermittently bathed in light by the sudden flashes. Death was approaching, the body wracked with pain, but the mind was still capable of thoughts. Time, like life itself, was ebbing away and they had to be expressed.

One of the thieves, even at that late stage, typical of the unregenerate, continued to think not of salvation but only of rescue. Quite literally as a final resort, he turned to Jesus once more. It was impossible, but one might as well make the attempt! Battling against the whine of the winds and mustering what strength remained, he cried out, '*If* thou be Christ, save thyself and us' (Luke 23:39). If! Within an arm's length the power of sin was being broken by the Son of God, but the man did not know it, and had he done so would not have believed it. So near, and yet so far away! His heart was as hard and embittered as it had been throughout the day; the fearful weather conditions which Providence had rained upon him made no difference. With deepening disdain for the one beside him, he placed himself beyond the reach of hope and died in his sins without it. There cannot be a more tragic experience known to man (John 8:21).

When the day had dawned it had seemed impossible that any good could spring from it, filled as it was intended to be with cruelty, anguish and terror. However, something mysterious was happening deep within it all — nothing less than a miracle. The 'dew' of God's grace had quietly moistened the soul of the other criminal (Hosea 14:5), an experience as moving now as it was then (Luke 23:40-43), and as a result he also had much to think about.

Hours earlier he too had sought rescue for its own sake (Matt. 27:44), but that was before the Creator had forced him to stare into the eye of the storm and learn the hard way the foolishness of not fearing him. Pounded as he was from all sides by nature's ferocious anger, the heavens above roaring and the earth beneath quaking, the wretched man's terror had made him search his heart. He did so that afternoon enveloped in the blackness of night, lonely and frightened, without any hope or apparent help.

Awesome majesty loomed over him, and he knew he was a lost soul. The Creator and Sustainer of all things is to be feared, an acknowledgement the thief had not made before. If God was capable of wreaking such havoc on Skull Hill, what could he do with one lawbreaking sinner? Jesus had once said something similar, although it is doubtful whether the thief had heard it: 'Fear him, which after he hath killed hath power to cast into hell: yea, I say unto you, Fear him' (Luke 12:5). Aware of divine holiness, his sinful life rising up to condemn him, the thief was eager to warn others.

He turned to his compatriot in crime. Did he not fear God? Then in a remarkable display of grace, he added, 'We receive the due reward of our deeds' (Luke 23:41). Not long before he had been an unrepentant criminal reviling Jesus; now he was admitting he deserved to be crucified! Not many could say that. God had revealed to him the righteousness of the law, under which he as a sinner had been cursed (Gal. 3:10), causing his soul to cry out in effect: 'O wretched man that I am! Who shall deliver me from the body of this death?' The answer was not far away. In the same position Paul said,

'I thank God through Jesus Christ our Lord' (Rom. 7:12,24,25). Unlike Paul, the thief did not understand theology but he nevertheless recognized his desperate need of Jesus.

But who was this unusual man from Nazareth? With many others that day he had heard the priests' 'sermon'. They had denied Jesus' claims to be the Son of God and the words written in three languages on Pilate's sardonic inscription nailed above Jesus' head: 'JESUS OF NAZARETH THE KING OF THE JEWS' (John 19:19), but the thief had been close to him for hours.

Throughout Jesus' ascent to Skull Hill and during his time upon the cross, the thief had witnessed his remarkable behaviour, his gracious submission to the brutality meted out to him and loving spirit to those around him, especially his love for his mother in entrusting her to John's care and protection (John 19:26-27). There was no mistaking the fact he had 'done nothing amiss'. Why, he had heard Jesus speaking to one he called 'Father', and asking that he would forgive his enemies (Luke 23:34). He was an enemy; there must therefore be hope, even for him!

The astonished man felt the gracious compulsion to speak to Jesus immediately. There must be no delay; the matter was urgent. But was he not too sinful? He was a thief, an outcast from the synagogue, without any good works to offer. Would he be accepted? Yet he knew Jesus had mixed with people like him (Matt. 9:10). Perhaps the story of Zacchæus, the crooked tax-gatherer, was also known to him. Even he became a follower of Jesus: 'This day is salvation come to this house... For the Son of man is come to seek and to save that which was lost' (Luke 19:9,10). There *was* hope! Had not Jesus bidden people like him, 'labouring' under the heavy burden of the law, to come to him to find rest for their souls? (Matt. 11:28-30).

The thief with dying eyes looked across at Jesus, but the darkness hid his features. Was it too late? Supposing he was already dead? He must make the supreme effort to speak to him, difficult though that would be with a swollen tongue and lips. With what energy was left the desperate sinner called out weakly, trusting the wind would carry his whispers in the right direction: 'Lord, remember me when

thou comest into thy kingdom' (Luke 23:42). Two of Jesus' disciples, aided by their mother, had coveted high rank in the heavenly
kingdom, but the thief, so aware of his own unworthiness, wanted
only to be remembered (Matt. 20:20-21).

The request was vague. There was much confusion in Israel
about the Messianic hope, with the Sadducees not believing in it at
all, but the Jews who did were all agreed over one thing: the
Messiah's arrival was over numerous hills, and many horizons
away. The thief's expectancy was therefore not high: if only the
Messiah would carry his name somewhere deep in his subconscious
when he eventually made his glorious appearance on the world's
stage once more. That was all, he could not expect anything else.

The man, so close to death, listened for any response there might
be, but was it too late? Suddenly, on the winds could be heard the
whispered response with the solemn emphasis for which Jesus was
known: 'Verily I say unto thee, Today shalt thou be with me in
paradise' (Luke 23:43) *Today!* Not something far off, nor a mere
glance from such an exalted figure, but the promise that he would
accompany the poor sinner into the heavenly park — today! Indeed,
he would be 'absent from the body ... present with the Lord' (2 Cor.
5:8) — an assurance shared by all possessors of saving faith.
Minutes later, the gates of the park opened wide, but not before Jesus
had had many thoughts of his own.

9.
Beyond the camp

The first three hours spent on the cross, from nine until noon, Jesus' sufferings were without question acute, his body bleeding profusely, bruised, disjointed and torn. Psalm 22 reveals how troubled his mind was: 'I am a worm, and no man; a reproach of men, and despised of the people. All they that see me laugh me to scorn... Be not far from me; for trouble is near; for there is none to help' (Ps. 22:6,11). He knew, though, that what was to follow would be worse, much worse, and very shortly it would grip him violently. The moments passed very slowly as he waited in trepidation for the inevitable.

It arrived at noon, signalled by the darkness which enveloped the entire land. With the suddenness of a light switched off, a darkness of a deeper hue enshrouded Jesus, as black despair gushed through every recess of his being and intensified with each minute of the succeeding three hours. His physical agony, terrible as it was, proved no match for this overwhelming experience, one he had not known before. He looked heavenwards for help, but none was forthcoming.

Atonement for the sins of men

The hours were only three, but the intensity of hell's white heat was eternal. Divine wrath poured over the Son, the spotless Lamb, as the Father's loathing of the least particle of sin waged the ultimate war against its dominion over the beloved flock whose place he was taking (John 10:11). Sins known and unknown, and those yet to be committed, made their way to him like metal filings to a magnet, each one dealt a withering blow, the slate wiped clean in the precious blood of the Redeemer (1 John 1:7).

He felt his soul dragged downwards into an ever-deepening crevice of wretched desolation and torment, where contact with heaven and humanity had withered and died. The full glare of perfect holiness, like raging flame (Heb. 12:29), engulfed it without any hint of mercy. Down, down, it soared in a vortex of vengeance, for which there was no respite or hope of surfacing (Luke 16:19-31). He was indeed 'stricken, smitten of God, and afflicted' (Isa. 53:4). Such was the violence when the terrors of divine holiness did battle with the devilish powers of sin, within the crumpled form of Jesus.

A Messianic cry was heard once more (Ps. 22:1): *'Eli, Eli, lama sabachthani?'*, as Jesus expressed his yearning for the comfort of his Father's companionship, but all he received in return, and that from a stranger, was a sponge soaked in sour wine (Matt. 27:46-48). It was not unexpected. His question had been rhetorical; it required no answering. For the first time the Father had turned his head away from his only begotten Son. He was forsaken, the heavens as black as the unfathomable pit through which his soul was hurtling. He understood that the beauty of holiness could not fellowship with the vileness of sin that he as the Lamb of God was carrying (2 Cor. 5:21). His wounds were the only way his people can know healing for theirs (Isa. 53:5).

Now they can answer Job's question: 'How should man be just with God?' (Job 9:2). By Jesus' blood his people are justified. The curse of the broken law was removed from them, because the Lamb received that curse in himself on their behalf (Gal. 3:10-13). Sin, which as a principle and a power bound them to Satan as a right, 'the power of darkness' (Col. 1:13), was broken for ever. Thus God's child, a guilty sinner at the bar of judgement, has heard the wonderful assurance from the Judge himself: 'Not guilty!' (Rom. 8:1). The reasons for that guilt have been erased. Another has taken his place under condemnation. The Father has not turned a 'blind eye' to sin; on the contrary, at Calvary the Son by one offering suffered the full consequences of it. As Adam was the representative head of the fallen human race (1 Cor. 15:22), the Son of God likewise took full responsibility for the salvation of his brethren and sisters (Heb. 2:9-18).

But what about Bildad's question: 'Or how can he be clean that is born of a woman?' (Job 25:4). It is one thing to declare the sinner 'not guilty', but how can he be welcomed into the presence of a sin-hating and righteous God, without being righteous ('clean') himself? Being without guilt is not to be equated with being righteous.

The answer once again is found on Skull Hill. As the justified sinner is no longer legally guilty in God's sight, he has also been declared righteous. Not that God's child possesses any natural virtue, but rather, he has the Spirit-directed conviction that his iniquity has been removed and has been clothed 'with [a] change of raiment' (Zech. 3:4-5). What a 'fair mitre' rests upon his head, a glorious 'crown of righteousness'! (2 Tim. 4:6-8). It is the 'fine linen' in which the bride of Christ is dressed, his righteousness put to their account (Rev. 19:8).

Thus God's people are 'accepted in the Beloved' (Eph. 1:6); that is, through their Redeemer, and only through him. They are accepted in time and throughout eternity, on the basis of the full atonement made at Calvary. It is a 'finished' work, and cannot be subtracted from, as in liberal theology, nor added to, as in Roman Catholicism (John 17:4). The redeemed, born again, justified and sanctified, stand before God everlastingly with heads lifted high and a song in their hearts, not the old song of nature (Rev. 4:11), but the 'new song' of grace (Rev. 5:9).

But how is a sinner reckoned to be justified? When he exercises a God-given saving faith (Rom. 5:1), trusting in the person and work of Christ as God the Son. Like Abraham, the 'father' of the faithful, he does not 'stagger' in unbelief (Rom. 4:20-25), but on the contrary 'believes God' who cannot lie (Heb. 6:18) and that is 'counted to him for righteousness' (Gen. 15:6).

'It is finished!'

It was mid-afternoon. Angry clouds, drifting swiftly from the scene, permitted the sun to bathe the land in warmth and light once more.

Lighted torches in every home were snuffed out, nature expressed its delight again and quietness settled over a rain-drenched Calvary. The terrifying storm had at last abated, leaving behind it a bedraggled remnant on Skull Hill: Jesus' devoted mother and her friends, exhausted soldiers and an astonished and converted centurion. His cry, 'Certainly this was a righteous man...' (Luke 23:47) '...the Son of God' (Mark 15:39), summed it all up.

Gazing at Jesus, broken and limp ('My strength is dried up like a potsherd; and my tongue cleaveth to my jaws,' Ps. 22:15), they saw his lips move and heard him speak with great difficulty but with triumphant finality: 'It is finished' (John 19:30). It was all over. Then, having committed his soul to the Father's safe-keeping, he closed his eyes and died (Luke 23:46).

Jesus would surely not have said that 'it' was 'finished' unless he wanted those at the scene, and the entire world, to know what 'it' was. There is a way of discovering the answer, if one appreciates that whatever was on Jesus' mind was rooted in the Scriptures, and to a particular aspect of them.

His thoughts would have wandered backwards in time, to the days long before when the Israelites encamped in the harsh desert. That was a period, saturated as it was in heaven's favour, that was never far from the Jewish mind, for so much that was eternally significant had taken place, from the declaration of the Decalogue to the establishing of the principles for divine worship through the erection of the tabernacle (Exod. 20-40). God's people were taught about the perfect purity of his character, the value of blood to appease his holy anger against human depravity and the only acceptable approach that sinners can make to him.

As each dawn broke over the silent Israelite encampment, the sound of trumpets awoke the people to the freshness of a new day. This was not reveille as once practised in an army camp. It was much more important than that. The silver trumpets were blown by the priests standing in the outer courtyard of the tabernacle, because they had watched as the ashes of the night's burnt offering had fallen through the brass grating of the altar. The sacrifice was completed; it was 'finished' (Lev. 6:9).

The Israelites appreciated what that meant. Not only had a new day begun, with its unique and exciting prospects, but it was a time of their 'gladness' (Num. 10:10), when the trumpet blasts heralded the news that God had accepted the offering which had been burning through the night. The phrase 'It is finished', then, was a triumphant trumpet call to the people of God that he was appeased and fully satisfied. In which case, they were safe from his angered displeasure.

However, they were safe for only a few hours. As the people stirred and the day gathered momentum, Aaron and his assistants were back at work in the courtyard. Theirs was an extremely busy daily schedule. No sooner had the shrill sounds of the trumpets died away than it was time for the morning sacrifice to take place. Aaron, his priestly sons and Levite assistants repeated what they had done the night before (Exod. 29:38-39). In other words, each day, seven days a week, two young lambs were offered to God as a burnt sacrifice upon the altar where flames continually leapt high (Lev. 6:8-9). There was never a break from this daily routine, for the appeasing of the righteous God was a task as continuous as the sinfulness of man itself.

At no time were the flames on the altar doused, even if they could have been, for they had descended from heaven (Lev. 9:23-24). In a very solemn ceremony, the inauguration of divine worship in the tabernacle had been accompanied by miraculous signs. The brothers, Moses and Aaron, had blessed the vast congregation of God's people gathered at the door of the tabernacle. Then the dazzling cloud of glory appeared, in which the divine presence was manifested to the entire assembly. No sooner had they recovered from this display of beatific splendour than fire suddenly gushed from the direction of the most holy place and settled upon the altar where the mangled flesh and bones of the sacrifice waited. The great God of glory had publicly, and miraculously, vindicated the 'blueprint' he had given to Moses (Exod. 25:8-9). In appreciation of that fact, and in awe of the occasion, the people had exulted and fallen to the ground in the spirit of adoration (Lev. 9:23-24).

The altar, then, stood in the centre of the tabernacle's outer courtyard and the flames danced continually upon it. Every day and night of the year, every year, they engulfed the constant stream of sacrificial offerings in a frenzied embrace until the charred remains disappeared through the brass grating, making room for its successor.

The tabernacle itself was central to the life of the people, and this was illustrated by the fact that the twelve tribes were encamped around it. At its heart stood, unseen, the ark of the covenant in the most holy place where God had promised to meet with his people at the mercy-seat which formed the lid of this most sacred box overlaid with gold (Exod. 25:22).

The burnt offering

Throughout each day, from the four parts of the encampment, a steady flow of people made their way to the only doorway of the outer courtyard, pulling what was probably an unwilling animal behind them. For those who could afford it this would have been a bullock or an ox (Lev. 1), but for most a lamb was sufficient. Like Mary and Joseph in later years, the very poor carried doves or pigeons (Luke 2:22-24).

These kinds of creatures had not been chosen arbitrarily by the owners, but by God himself (Lev. 1:2). Nor were the animals themselves picked at random, but each of them had been especially examined before being taken from the pen or cage. For the burnt offering, they had to be male yearlings and without any physical blemish at all (Exod. 12:5). The reason for this is evident. They symbolized the Lamb of God being led to the slaughter, and to the heart of the flames as a sacrifice for sin.

Once at the door of the tabernacle, the creature stood before its owner and one of the priests. It felt the former's hand placed heavily upon its head, the sinner and the sacrifice closely identified with each other, and with this symbolic gesture the owner's confessed sin had been made over to it in the sight of God (Lev. 1:3-4) The animal was then led into the courtyard, as the owner's divinely appointed substitute, to be prepared for sacrifice as in the presence of the living God. The sharpness of the knife, drawn swiftly across the creature's throat, produced the necessary flow of warm blood which filled the bowl carried by the priest. Here was a life poured forth on behalf of the sinner, for 'The life of the flesh is in the blood' (Lev. 17:11).

The priest then continued with the solemn proceedings. He took the bowl and liberally sprinkled the blood on all sides of the altar, as well as upon it, signifying the universal appeal of the sacrifice (Lev. 1:5). With hundreds of such incidents taking place each day, the thick carpet of blood squelched as the priests walked to and fro through it. Blood was the predominant feature of the tabernacle, as it was at Calvary — the blood of the atoning sacrifice.

The creature was then flayed, preferably by the sinner, for there was nothing superficial about this moment. It was hard work, and God wanted the sinner to realize it, in anticipation of the profound ministry his Son would exercise upon Skull Hill centuries later. There was nothing superficial about nails hammered into flesh, or the tormented soul of the Son of God.

It also took time before the task was completed, and each part of the offering was divided according to the law (Lev. 1:12). The skin was ripped open and pulled free from the carcase, the head and legs severed from the body and the innards and fat cut from the bones. Not only was the sinner reminded of the profundity of atonement, but also of the abyss of sin's depravity. Like a hidden mineshaft in every soul, its depth can only be measured by God himself. In other words, imputed sin was not lying gently on the offering's remains, but deep within. By the same token, it could not be wiped away as with a cloth. The sharp knife was plunged into the mass of flesh, cutting and slicing as it manoeuvred its way to the bone in the hands of an expert.

A few feet away from where the altar stood was a large bronze water container, the laver (Exod. 30:18), to which a priest carried the legs and the intestines of the burnt offering for washing (Lev. 1:9). Again, strict symbolism was being observed. If the sinner had to pass the altar before reaching the laver, personal salvation always preceding sanctification, the burnt offering was always washed before being placed upon the altar, signifying Christ's overall purity before bearing the sins of others.

The washing having been completed, the sacrifice was ready to be offered to God as 'a sweet savour' (Lev. 1:9). As it was prophesied of the Messiah that 'His visage was so marred more than any man, and his form more than the sons of men' (Isa. 52:14), so by this time the offering on the altar was unrecognizable. It was a reminder, both to the priest and to the sinner standing nearby, of the havoc sin wreaks upon the soul and of the enormous consequences to the Saviour who dealt it the fatal blow. Those present at Calvary witnessed the truth of this.

Nothing could illustrate the sufferings of Christ more fully than the portrait of the priests busy at the altar of burnt offering, their faces streaming with sweat caused by the blistering heat of the desert sun and the scorching ferocity of the heavenly flames which roared skywards close by. Each part of the offering was laid in an orderly fashion on the wood already engulfed in fire: the head, the 'fat', intestines and the legs. The Lamb of God was not spared: the head and 'fat' symbolizing the external and internal aspects of his being, and the intestines and legs the inner and outer purity of his nature.

The mangled flesh and bone of the burnt offering, the 'type' and anticipation of the Lamb of God, was carefully placed by the priest among the flames. There was nothing haphazard, or careless, about his action. He understood that God, who 'spared not his own Son' (Rom. 8:32), demanded the sacrifice to be in the centre of the fire, at the hottest part of the conflagration, over the brass grating through which the ashes would fall.

The flesh saturated in blood and water, as Jesus' body was at Calvary, especially after the spear had pierced it (John 19:34), began at first to sizzle its discomfort in the 'Golgotha' of the intense heat. Before long, however, the flames licked the offering dry of all moisture ('I thirst', cried the Lamb) and its short-lived unease surrendered to the inevitability of the fiery embrace.

Soon, the blackened, charred embers dissolved into an unrecognizable heap which gradually edged its way through the grating and vanished from sight. The head of the sacrifice the sinner had leaned upon not long before, which had borne his sin and guilt, had disappeared from sight and would never be seen again. The atonement was completed; it was 'finished', and time for rejoicing.

The odour of burning flesh hung like a cloud over the entire tribal encampment, every hour of day and night, an unmistakable smell which would have proved intolerable had not the reasons for it been appreciated. Throughout each day of the years spent in the desert, the people saw smoke rising from the flaming fingertips in the courtyard of the tabernacle, curling upwards towards the blue sky, and knew that it reached deeply into the nostrils of their God. The continual scent which permeated every tent day and night, a 'sweet savour unto the Lord' (Lev. 1:9), was a constant reminder that he was delighted with his people. A covenant people, rooted and grounded in blood sacrifice, must of necessity be a 'special people unto himself, above all people that are upon the face of the earth' (Deut. 7:6). The 'finished' work of the atoning sacrifice served to underline this fact.

It was for this reason that Jesus laid such stress upon the completion of his sacrificial work (John 17:4), even to crying out the fact seconds before his death (John 19:30). It has always been vital for a child of the covenant, whether Hebrew or Christian, to learn that an atonement has been made for his soul (Lev. 17:11). As the Old Testament believer returned home, knowing that the burnt sacrifice had been entirely consumed in the fierce flames, how contented he must have been! His sin and guilt, although not washed away (Heb. 10:4), were at least 'covered' until the next time.

The tabernacle courtyard, so close to the sacred spot where the ark of the covenant stood in silent testimony to the holiness of God, was no place where he would desire to linger even if permitted to do so. He had witnessed the solemnity of the priests, seen the sharp knife in operation, felt the heat of the fire and heard the hiss of burning flesh and bone — all this, in the process of appeasing the divine displeasure. The man deserved the condemnation it symbolized, but a bullock, lamb or turtle doves and pigeons had borne the brunt instead. It was cause for rejoicing. How much more so for those whose sacrifice was never penned or caged behind their tents, but is the Son of the living God from heaven!

The meat offering

However, Jesus' thoughts during those hours on the cross could
have penetrated further than the burnt offering, important though it
was. He was also the fulfilment of the other offerings: the meat,
peace, sin, trespass and drink offerings. Each had its particular
meaning.

When the Hebrew arrived back at his tent, his next visit to the
tabernacle was already being prepared by his wife. It was the meat
offering, which always accompanied the burnt offering, or followed
soon after. It symbolized the grateful dedication of the sinner to
God, his entire life and all his possessions, as a result of his having
been forgiven. For this reason the meat offering could never precede
the other, for it is impossible for the unrepentant to commit their
lives to God.

The meat offering always consisted of three ingredients, the
main one being *fine flour* which had been shaken vigorously in the
sieve, and the other two were oil and frankincense (Lev. 2:1). As the
man made his way for the second time to the tabernacle, he knew he
carried with him a highly valued treasure in God's sight. This was,
firstly, because like the burnt offering, the accompanying meat
offering also had Christ as its central theme. What 'finer flour' could
there be than a life strenuously sifted by the hand of God and placed
under the microscope of the moral, ceremonial and judicial laws —
and found to be sinless? (John 8:46). The righteous demands of
those laws were met in Jesus, in whom heaven witnessed the
intensity of love for God and man expected of all (Matt. 22:36-40).

Upon the flour was poured *oil*, the sign of anointing by the Holy
Spirit and the separation to God and his service which results from
it (1 Sam. 16:13). With crowds lining the banks of the River Jordan
as witnesses, Jesus had entered the water for baptism in a public
acknowledgement that his ministry had officially begun. Immediately after the ceremony, as Jesus was ascending the riverbank once
more, the Spirit came upon him and the Father's voice was heard
delighting in his Son (Matt. 3:13-17). This remarkable experience
was the fulfilment of a promise made in heaven, before time began,
when God the Father anticipated the beauty of Christ's purity and

grace upon earth and anointed him 'with the oil of gladness above [his] fellows' (Heb. 1:9).

Then sprinkled upon the flour was the *frankincense*, one of the precious gifts given to the infant Jesus by the wise men (Matt. 2:11). It symbolized adoration and deity. If the burnt offering witnessed to the *work* of the Son of God, the meat offering pointed to his *person*. The one who entered the heart of the conflagration was none other than God himself in the perfection of his nature, bathed in eternal glory, and separated for humble ministry among men (Matt. 20:28).

The bearer of the meat offering, had he been capable of realizing it, was, for another reason, in possession of the symbol denoting the greatest gift known to the repentant sinner. That is to know God intimately in time and to bask in divine beneficence as he anticipates the promised everlasting splendour (John 17:24). The whiteness of the refined flour, the pouring of the oil and the sprinkling of frankincense, each told its own story.

Years after the events at Calvary the apostle John was granted a glorious vision of the triumphant Christ, Lord of all and Ruler of the nations. However, the Victor is not alone. Behind him marches an equally victorious army, paraded in the most beautiful of uniforms that match his own: 'fine linen, white and clean' (Rev. 19:14). The imputed righteousness of Christ, without which a sinner is devoid of hope (2 Cor. 5:21), is the best of reasons why he desires to offer his 'meat offering' and surrender everything he is and has to the Captain of his salvation (Heb. 2:10). Dressed in such pure apparel, with the anointing 'oil' of new birth and the 'frankincense' of an adoring heart, the Christian's constant delight is to emulate the example of his Redeemer in ready obedience and sacrificial service to the living God.

The peace offering

But Jesus' thoughts during those long hours were not only about his suffering, the fulfilment of the ancient burnt and meat offerings. He knew that his 'finished' work at Calvary related to the peace offering too (Lev. 3:1). These three close companions were never divided, and they always followed each other in that order. If the burnt offering symbolized the atoning sacrifice of the Lamb of God, and the meat offering his absolute dedication to the divine will (John 5:30), the peace offering signified the joyful thanksgiving which resulted from the other two.

Jesus might well have silently quoted the psalmist, for he would have known the words well: 'I will offer to thee the sacrifice of thanksgiving, and will call upon the name of the Lord' (Ps. 116:17). A few hours before he had spoken to his disciples about his joy, that they might experience the fulness of it (John 15:11). Jesus was certainly 'a man of sorrows, and acquainted with grief' (Isa. 53:3), but beyond the cross lay the crown! (Heb. 12:2).

Despite the raging of nature hurling itself at Calvary (Ps. 18:4-17) — a black velvet sky, thunderous noises, lightning flashing, whirling winds, rains and hailstones — who was in a better position than the Lamb to provide the 'peace offering' of thanksgiving? The Sacrifice, torn and bleeding under the 'knife' wielded by the Father, nevertheless looked heavenwards. Jesus could 'see' heaven's gates opening ready to receive the sinners for whom he was being sacrificed.

Not long afterwards, the first Christian martyr witnessed a similar scene: 'the Son of man standing on the right hand of God' (Acts 7:56). How much more clearly would that same Son of man have been able to 'see' the Father seated on his throne of grace and glory? Bloodied but not bowed, with the words of Psalm 22 uppermost in his mind (Matt. 27:46), he prayed. The inaudible Messianic prayer pierced the oppressive gloom: 'My praise shall be of thee in the great congregation: I will pay my vows before them that fear him' (Ps. 22:25). No greater congregation could there have been than that which observed the Saviour's 'vows' being paid in full.

The searching power of God's light

But even the few loyal supporters who gathered at the foot of his cross would not have been capable of defining the depth to which the 'knife' had been plunged into the sacrificial Lamb. One thing is certain: God's ways are never superficial. When the offerings at the tabernacle required flaying, sharp knives and clenched fists tore the skin from the carcase. Likewise, when the 'fat' and the intestines were removed, the knife plunged deeply into the mass of tissue.

In other words, whereas sinners are tempted to be bland when contemplating their sinfulness, God searches for the least speck of sin 'deep down'. As the prophet heard him declare, 'I the Lord search the heart' (Jer. 17:10). He therefore instigated the sin and trespass offerings to cover that eventuality. As the hymnist reminds us,

> Eternal Light! Eternal Light!
> How pure the soul must be,
> When placed within thy searching sight...

It is only when the searching begins that a sinner has any possibility of understanding what took place at Calvary, and what Jesus meant when he stated that 'it' was 'finished'.

For example, the day Jesus 'suffered without the gate' (Heb. 13:12) sin was as much in evidence as the presence of Satan. It manifested itself in Pilate's injustice, the barbarity of the mobs, the viciousness of the soldiers, the shaking fists of the priests and above all in that which the Saviour bore in himself on behalf of others. Nobody who reads the account of what transpired then can mistake the fact that wickedness was rampant in every direction, from the Roman and Jewish authorities to the lowliest soldier and man in the street.

However, the light of God penetrated beneath the obvious. It searched for the shady corners in the less expected places, where lurked some surprises among those claiming allegiance to his Son. Only he, and heaven itself, failed to be shocked by what the light revealed: sly treachery for a few silver coins, hypocrisy, proud boasts, lies, cowardly denials and the sounds of running feet as those for whom Christ was appointed to die left him in the lurch. Without reference to the three years Jesus and his apostles had walked

together, the catalogue of shame took place within the space of a few
hours the previous evening.

Yet even as Jesus reflected upon it all, during the hours of
desolation, he was making sure that each individual sin of his people
was in the process of being erased through his flowing and cleansing
sacrificial blood. Of those who had scurried away in the darkness,
leaving behind a trail of broken promises (Matt. 26:35), only John
remained to hear the welcomed news: 'It is finished.' God had freely
forgiven them, root and branch, and had even forgotten every detail
of their sinful failures. Had they understood that night what 'it' was
that had 'finished', the apostles (except the tragic Judas) could have
prayed beside their beds delighting in the grace of God promised
through Isaiah seven hundred years earlier: 'O Lord, I will praise
thee: though thou wast angry with me, thine anger is turned away,
and thou comfortedst me' (Isa. 12:1).

Still the light continued piercing the gloom, as it turned its
attention to that for which the sin and trespass offerings were made
available (Lev. 4-7). The laws were plain: they reminded the
individual of his proneness to sin against God and his neighbour.
Such is the power of the sin principle, and the deceitfulness of the
human heart (Jer. 17:9) that sins are allowed to permeate and corrupt
without any declaration of intent. Sinners are aware of their existence, but have no idea of their depth.

With impunity, sins are committed against God without the culprit even being aware of them. Hence the sin offering catered for this
all-too-frequent occurrence. Similarly, sins were committed against
one's neighbour in thought, word and deed of which only God was
aware. The trespass offering supplied that need. Thus, with the five
major sacrificial offerings (the burnt, meat, peace, sin and trespass),
God's perfect purity was vindicated and his anger appeased.

It was left to Christ to pay the full penalty in the sight of heaven,
not just for sins in general, but for the minutiæ of sin's particles in
each of his people through the ages. The 'mineshaft' had not only to
be emptied of its murky contents, but washed clean of the least flake
of dirt and grime. It is only the power of Christ's atoning blood
which can deliver sinners from the authority of satanic darkness into
which they were born (Col. 1:13-14).

How often Jesus must have been aware of the secret sins against heaven and humanity in those around him! Only one who was himself devoid of the sin principle, who could challenge others (John 8:46) and even Satan to search vainly for it within him (John 14:30), could notice the unpleasant and ungodly facets of others' hearts that were normally kept hidden from view (Mark 2:8). For thirty years Jesus had lived under the same roof as Mary and Joseph, and for much of that period with their children (Mark 6:3), and during that time he had been capable of 'knowing their thoughts' (Matt. 9:4). How disconcerting it was! How uneasy they felt at times! Small wonder that, with Jesus' growth into manhood and with his spiritual sensitivity sharpening, those nearest to him turned against him (Mark 3:21).

That eternal light of God, clear as crystal (Rev. 4:6), shone brilliantly through the Son without wavering. In fact, he is the light (John 12:46), as he is also the way, the truth and the life (John 14:6). Jesus could read the human heart and mind as others read books. Nathanael quickly learned this upon being introduced to Jesus, when he was informed that he had already been quietly observed and 'seen'. Nathanael had no doubt what was implied, and expressed his astonishment: 'Rabbi, thou art the Son of God; thou art the King of Israel' (John 1:48-49). Not only Nathanael, but all the apostles felt the penetrating purity of their Lord's gaze. He knew Judas was a 'devil' even before he chose him as an apostle (John 6:70-71), read the yearning of the disciples' hearts for prominence in his kingdom (Luke 9:46-47), fathomed Peter's pride with warnings of denials and broke the brittle boastings of them all by foretelling their forth-coming disloyalty to him (Matt. 26:31-35). In short, as the psalmist succinctly puts it, 'He that formed the eye, shall he not see?' (Ps. 94:9). Jesus' grief and disappointment must surely have been constant, realizing what man would have been but for his fall in Eden.

The Lamb of God bears the sins of his people

Yet despite this, it was the Shepherd's everlasting love for his flock which was the compelling force behind his appearance at Calvary

(John 10:11). They, like their brethren and sisters since, disappointed and dismayed him continually, but divine love never falters (John 10:27-29). God loved; therefore he gave (John 3:16). He had no intention of sparing his own Son, but would place him on the altar of sacrifice (Rom. 8:32), that righteousness might be vindicated, the sin principle dealt a final blow (Rom. 3:25) and Satan's power destroyed (Heb. 2:14).

In turn the Son volunteered to do the Father's will (Ps.40:6-9), the ancient offerings being unable to deal effectually with sin, and entered the world that he might rescue the elect who lay helpless and bound. There was only one way in which he could do it — by becoming flesh and blood as they were (John 1:14). In their midst, he looked heavenwards and testified to the Father, 'I will declare thy name unto my brethren, in the midst of the church will I sing praise unto thee' (Heb. 2:12). These were the children the Father had given to him, blood-washed believers of every age, those for whom he gave his life.

The Lamb of God had been led to the appointed venue, and had felt the hands of the elect pressing upon him in an act of identification. Like the high priest of old, wearing the breastplate in which were twelve jewels representing each tribe of Israel (Exod. 28:29), the Lamb was concerned compassionately for each single believer for whom his life's blood, the blood of the everlasting covenant, would be poured out. Not one could be overlooked whose name had been mentioned in the eternal council and written in the Lamb's book of life even before the dawn of history (Rev. 21:27). King or commoner, rich or poor, man or woman, adult or child, Jew or Gentile: heaven would be filled with the elect from both the old as well as the new dispensations. In heaven, the Lamb is the pivot around which everyone revolves and the cause for the singing of redemption's song of glory (Rev. 5:9).

With the erection of the cross, the Christ of God was slowly made aware as the hours passed of a depth of anguish far outweighing his physical sufferings, and one which he had not known before. He had been expecting it, for it was for this moment that he had been born.

Blackness of the deepest hue descended upon his soul as sin in all its loathsomeness swathed it. Sins, merely 'covered' (Ps. 32:1) by various legal offerings (Ps. 40:6), rose up from the depths of ancient times and filled the soul of Christ (Rom. 3:25) as they had been directed to do by God. Sins, too, which had already been committed, in thought, word and deed, by Jesus' contemporaries, and those which were yet to be conceived until the end of time, flew to the cross and found a similar dwelling-place. A fearful spirit of isolation gripped his soul, as he was 'made sin' (2 Cor. 5:21), causing him to shout out, as one ultimately desolate, 'My God, my God, why hast thou forsaken me?' (Matt. 27:46).

The sacrificial Lamb of God had been ripped open and 'flayed' by the almighty hands of the Father, his 'knife' slicing and cutting to the bone, in order to reach the least particle of sin tissue. The fierce light of burning holiness searched every recess of Christ's soul and the Father wreaked vengeance at will, without respite or mercy, against everything he found there. The power of 'cancelled sin' had been broken at last, the sinner set free.

In short, the Lamb was experiencing the torments of eternal retribution that the elect deserved. The 'terrors of law and of God', as the hymn-writer put it, were felt that day by the Son because sinners had dared to break the moral law without restraint, offending the holy God (James 2:10). By Christ's passive obedience on the cross, both God and his commandments were satisfied. At the same time, Satan and sin were dealt a blow from which there could be no recovery, and satanic principalities were overthrown triumphantly (Col. 2:14-15). It was the moment when a drink offering was called for, to pour over the offering in a demonstration of one's gratitude to the Almighty (1 Sam. 1:24).

The 'altar flames', having leaped high around the soul of Christ for hours, the burning 'heat' of eternal wrath having reached its fullest intensity, the Lamb of God experienced what was unique to himself. As the final and smallest fragments of the sacrificial offerings had at one time slithered through the grating of the altar of burnt offering, the figure hanging limply upon the cross had reached his lowest ebb. Christ had given everything, his being sapped of all strength, for he could not give more than his life. His blood had been poured out into the fountain for 'sin and for uncleanness' (Zech. 13:1).

The moment Jesus whispered, 'It is finished' (John 19:30), heaven was filled with a paean of praise and every recess resounded to everlasting songs of exultation. It was the eternal 'day of gladness' when 'silver trumpets' blew (Num. 10:9-10) in grateful recognition that Christ's work was completed and that God had made his peace with sinners (Luke 2:14).

The dawn of a new day

Jerusalem was swathed in the half-light of dawn, soon to awake to a new day. The tip of the sun would shortly appear above the horizon, and swiftly sweep the darkness of night away. It could not arrive too soon for most of the citizens, who had been awoken early by the sounds of a distant but powerful earth tremor (Matt. 28:2). The narrow streets and dingy alleyways, normally quiet at such an hour except for the occasional barking of dogs, were quickly filled with chattering people.

This had not been the first earthquake in recent times. Calvary, that gruesome place, had suffered one a few days earlier. In fact, during the previous seventy-two hours or so Jerusalem had become accustomed to the abnormal and frightening. The weather conditions had been atrocious, the worst in living memory (Ps. 18:4-15), including a fearful and intense darkness covering not only the city, but the entire land (Matt. 27:45). If that was not enough, quite a few graves in the local cemetery had mysteriously opened — and were now empty! (Matt. 27:52-53).

There was also a report that something fearful had taken place in the heart of the temple at the very time Jesus of Nazareth had died. That sacred area, the most holy place, to which only the high priest had access, and that just once a year (Heb. 9:7) on the Day of Atonement (Lev. 16), was exposed. The veil hiding it from public view had been torn from the top to the bottom by an unseen hand (Matt.

27:50-51). Long before, Aaron's two eldest sons had been struck down by God for their unworthiness on this side of the richly embroidered curtain (Lev. 10:1-2), but now it was ripped in two anyone was capable of seeing beyond it — a captital offence under the old dispensation (Lev. 16:2). How the people must have trembled! Yet they were also puzzled, for God remained silent. Nothing happened!

At the time, no one made the connection between the death of Jesus and the tearing of the veil, but following the powerful descent of God the Spirit on the Day of Pentecost (Acts 2) when the primitive church had the truth revealed to it (John 16:13), the wonderful realization dawned. The events on Skull Hill, far from being the dismal anticlimax they appeared to be (Luke 24:18-21), were in fact the triumphant fulfilment of centuries of anticipation.

On the cross Jesus had lain passively in the hand of the Father, meekly obedient in his appalling sufferings. To the spectators the experience had appeared negative, with nothing good arising out of it, from the anguish of the agony sustained to the anger expressed in the heavens. When the distressing hours had at last ended, and Skull Hill was vacated, there was rejoicing in Jerusalem in the corridors of priestly power. Israel had seen the last of the Galilean carpenter. It was all over — or was it? They little realized what problems lay ahead for them (Acts 2-4).

In fact the torn veil signified yet another irony: the irrelevance of Caiaphas as high priest and his colleagues on the council. God had declared them redundant! He had observed the heckling and mockery of his dying Son and had heard their 'sermon' from the mound, and the situation called for the reminder that 'Before destruction the heart of man is haughty, and before honour is humility' (Prov. 18:12). Calvary marked their 'destruction' and Jesus' 'honour'.

They were unaware of the greatness of the occasion, and would not have believed it had they known, but even as they reviled Jesus the true Day of Atonement was taking place a few feet from them. Despairing though his death appeared to be, had they the ears to hear, they would have heard the shouts of acclamation as heaven's High Priest entered the most sacred of all places (Rev. 5). He had no

need to do it annually; just once was sufficient — and how careful
God is to differentiate between 'once' and 'often'! (Heb. 7; 9).
Christ is the only priest sinners require, the one with nail prints in his
hands, whose redemptive authority assures the penitent of salvation
'to the uttermost' (Heb. 7:25).

Nor did he carry a bowl filled with animal blood; it was his own
blood that paved the way, and he wore no breastplate with the
famous twelve jewels, each one of which represented an Israelite
tribe (Exod. 28:29). Instead, far more intimately, he carried in his
heart the name of every member of his flock (Heb. 6:18-20).
Through the 'veil' of his flesh he took them (and once was sufficient), a kingdom of priests (Rev. 1:6) with holy boldness to
approach God (Heb. 4:15-16) 'the fountain of living waters' (Jer.
17:13) in the name of the great High Priest and through the merits
of his blood (1 Peter 1:18-19).

Who would not envy them? They are the greatest 'success story'
history has known, conquerors and much more besides. The King
smiles upon his subjects; the Redeemer loves his redeemed; the
High Priest honours his priests; the Shepherd cherishes his flock.
The two parties are inseparable, whatever the circumstances,
whether in time or eternity (Rom. 8:35-39). He has always loved
them, entered the world to rescue them, made atonement for their
souls and now by his 'unchangeable priesthood' (Heb. 7:24) everlastingly intercedes for them from the right hand of the majestic
throne in glory (Heb. 1:1-3).

But are they not pathetically few in number, and does the world
not have cause to scoff? God alone possesses 'the books' of heaven
and hell (Dan. 7:10) and his Son the keys (Rev. 1:18), but one
assumes that those who eternally wail outnumber those who eternally praise. That admitted, paradise harbours more saints than the
stars in the heavens (Gen. 15:5), and the multitudes surrounding
God's throne are innumerable (Rev. 7:9). Who in fact can possibly
'declare his generation'? (Isa. 53:8).

The beginning...

A figure stood amidst the shadows which overcast another beautiful tree-lined and luxuriant garden close to Calvary. The quiet stillness was broken only by birdsong. An empty tomb was nearby (John 19:41), the huge boulder which had sealed the opening flung to one side as if by powerful arms, while across the centuries could be heard Isaiah's song of jubilation: 'He will swallow up death in victory; and the Lord God will wipe away tears from all faces; and the rebuke of his people shall he take away from off all the earth' (Isa. 25:8).

Epilogue:
The day of the dry tree

The prelude to the disaster began in May of A. D. 66. What had for many years been merely disgruntled conversations about the Roman occupation of Israel, coupled with a limited number of flare-ups led by men from the same mould as Barabbas, grew into a confident desire for revenge with the tension reaching fever pitch. The Romans exacerbated the situation by treating the Jews with their usual disdain and when Procurator Florus, one of Pilate's successors, demanded seventeen talents from the temple treasury it brought matters to a head. The Jews replied by refusing to offer their daily sacrifices to the emperor, an action the Romans considered treasonable and an open declaration of war against the empire.

This fact in no way curbed the fanatical behaviour of the zealots who, with their increasing audacity and daring, became the talking-point of Rome itself. Gradually their cloak-and-dagger activities started taking effect, from darkened alleyway assassinations to the eventual defeat of an entire Roman legion. Success begat success, with the rebels gaining fresh recruits as the mighty Roman Empire was seen to be increasingly on the defensive. Soon the Roman garrison in Jerusalem was overrun, with Florus under so much pressure that he was obliged to seek the aid of the Roman legion stationed as far away as Syria. When it came, supplemented by auxilliary troops, the Jews routed their enemies. Nero in Rome decided to respond to the challenge.

In Britain at the time was an outstanding Roman general commanding the Second Legion (the Augusta), who under Claudius, a mere thirteen years or so after the crucifixion, had performed brilliant work in subduing the Britons. His name was Titus Flavius Vespasianus, and he was ordered to sail immediately with the legion to Israel where he took command of the entire Roman army. At his side was his twenty-eight-year-old son, Titus, who was to play such a significant role in the fulfilment of Jesus' prophecy (Luke 23:29-30, see chapter 8).

By October 67 the resistance in Galilee, where a generation earlier Jesus had walked, was crushed amidst fearful carnage. As a master race, Rome was in no mood to be embarrassed any more by Jewish audacity. Thousands of Jews were massacred, and those who survived were shipped off to Corinth as slaves to join Nero's building programme, the Corinth canal. A few months later Vespasian's legion (Vespasianus) was prepared for an onslaught upon Judæa.

While Jerusalem's citizens waited for the inevitable invasion, news reached the advancing Romans of their emperor's death. Nero's demise was not lamented, even by his family, but it presented problems for the leadership in awaiting a successor. As a result, the expected blood-letting took place in Rome. It was as well for Vespasian that he was occupied in a foreign land and avoided the political strife, for after three emperors had come and gone in quick succession the empire awoke to discover it had another, namely Vespasian. With his departure for Rome he handed over the military reins to his son Titus.

Titus was only thirty years old, but with his father sitting astride the empire the young man's confidence grew, bolstered as it was by the size of the army he controlled. This was enormous, and Rome could have been charged with overreacting to the Jewish rebels trapped within Jerusalem's walls. Four legions, the Fifth (Macedonia), Tenth (Fretensis), Twelfth (Fulminata) and the Fifteenth (Apollinaris), together with an assortment of auxilliary troops and cavalry, encamped close to the city. In all it comprised over 30,000 men, the most fearful and powerful fighting force Judæa had seen even in her wartorn history. It was the spring of A. D. 70, one generation after Jesus wept over Jerusalem and a date which was to linger in the memory of historians since (Luke 19:41-44). A bloodbath was awaiting those who found themselves besieged.

The assault begins

Jerusalem was packed with people, multitudes having arrived for the passover feast from all over the empire. However, tragically, the fighting began not from outside the city but from within it. With Jerusalem surrounded by hosts of combat-hardened and merciless warriors alerted for attack, the atmosphere behind the city walls was electric, but there was no closing of ranks among the Jews as one might have expected in the circumstances. On the contrary, like caged animals, fanatical factions began open warfare among themselves so that even before one Roman blade had flashed in the sunlight Jewish dead and wounded lay where they fell and their blood trickled through the streets. It was a prelude to the carnage which followed. Even the granaries stocked full of essential food supplies were razed to the ground in the civil war.

An aerial view of the scene would have looked impressive, with Jerusalem's massive and apparently impregnable walls standing invitingly before the mighty hordes of Imperial Rome, for whom such situations were commonplace wherever they had conquered. The Tenth Legion was encamped upon the Mount of Olives, covering the city's eastern flank, whilst Titus remained with the other three on Mount Scopus to the north-east. Jerusalem was secured in a vice-like grip from which there appeared to be no possibility of escape for the hapless victims. Titus called upon them to surrender, but their leaders on the city walls, although observing the fearful scene, scorned his appeal. He gave the order to attack, at which Roman military efficiency slotted easily into place.

Jerusalem consisted of four sections, each with its own wall, the most important being the temple area, to the south of which was the old town, built on the spur of steep cliffs on three of its sides, preventing the possibility of invasion. The new town was situated north of the temple, and between the two, as its name implies, was the middle town adjoining it. Within five days from the onslaught of the three legions which had advanced from Scopus, both the new and middle towns were overcome. The warfare was then concentrated upon what was left of the holy city, especially the area held most sacred by the Jews.

Once again the heavy weapons were trundled into position by a contingent of Roman soldiers expert at their task, and these were in constant use throughout the strife. First came the catapults for firing rocks ('ballista') or metal bolts ('catapulta'), fearsome war machines capable of creating immeasurable damage to buildings and, worse, horrific injuries to people. Nowhere in the city could a person feel safe, as boulders like cannon-balls and heavy sharp-pointed bolts flew over the high walls from various directions in an arbitrary manner. Property was smashed and people squashed to pulp, or pierced through with the metal arrows they had probably not even seen approaching.

The battering rams accompanied the catapults in the front line of the battle, and were in use along the main stretch of wall. In more primitive times soldiers had battered down hindrances by using tree-trunks, but the Assyrians and Greeks had perfected the technique by covering the ramming device with heavy timber in the shape of a hut. In this way the soldiers working it were protected from their enemies on the walls above them. The ram swung on thick ropes suspended from the ceiling of the hut, with the iron-plated end, designed in the shape of a ram's head, protruding through the wall at one end. When the hut was pushed on its wooden wheels towards the object of its attack it proved a formidable weapon.

Continuing resistance by the Jews

By the beginning of May in that momentous year of A. D. 70, after incessant bombardment by boulders and bolts and the monotonous battering upon the walls day and night, the Jews persisted in their resistance. Titus must have wondered what he had to do to overthrow them. He tried psychological warfare. Abandoning an all-out attack, he commanded his thousands of legionaries to muster for a grand parade in front of their curious enemies watching the spectacle from what was left of Jerusalem's defences.

The charade lasted for four days in an exhibition of Roman might and grandeur, with the brandishing of the legions' standards carrying the imprint of the Roman eagle. On the fifth day, Titus ordered a prominent Jewish captive, Flavius Josephus (from whom we have obtained the eyewitness account of the events), to make an appeal to his countrymen to surrender. Despite his touching appeals to Jewish sentiment and history, Jerusalem's remaining and stubborn inhabitants refused to comply with his wishes. With the pride of empire at stake, Titus restarted the war.

In July, it did not take long for his troops to burst into the Castle of Antonia. Ramps were built in an attempt to scale the final wall which stood between them and the temple close by, where the Jews were making a last-ditch stand. The Romans were not having it all their own way. Every effort to bridge the wall was met with courageous and sacrificial attempts by desperate and starving men to foil what they must have known was a hopeless situation. Many Jews managed to escape under cover of darkness over the walls and through subterranean passages, but their efforts invariably led to disaster. They were either killed outright, or if captured were crucified on the neighbouring hillsides. In fact, as the terrible drama continued to unfold an increasing number within Jerusalem surrendered their hold on reason and crawled to the Romans, knowing what the consequences would be. Soon the woodlands were bare and the hillsides peppered with crosses as five hundred crucifixions took place each day.

Surrounded on all sides

Titus was not satisfied. What may have seemed to him at first as a straightforward campaign was quickly becoming a personal nightmare. He had tried open and pyschological warfare but the success rate was proving expensive in terms of time, manpower and, not least, embarrassment. Knowing the civil war within the city had cost the Jews much of their food supply, he therefore decided to increase the pressure by starving them into submission, or death. He ordered the erection of a *circumvallatio*, an earthen wall surrounding Jerusalem, hermetically sealing it and cutting it off from any outside influence. Day and night the legionaries toiled and the work continued uninterrupted until it was completed. Titus was unaware he was fulfilling a prophecy first uttered ten years before his birth: 'For the days shall come upon thee, that thine enemies shall cast a trench about thee, and compass thee round, and keep thee in on every side' (Luke 19:43).

If the Jews had found ways and means of smuggling in small quantities of food before the building of the wall, all hope had now gone. Famine bit deeply into the last vestiges of courage and nobility, with abject despair and starvation taking their toll. The scenes within the city quickly degenerated, human depravity being exposed in its most stark and savage state, as Josephus recorded at the time. All sense of decency and propriety was forgotten as the victims hunted for food in packs like dogs, seeking the smallest morsel for themselves and killing those who stood in their way. Vicious fights broke out in the frantic struggle to stay alive, and those who appeared less gaunt than the rest were killed in the belief that they were harbouring food, whilst parents snatched it from their children's mouths.

Famine is, like death, a great leveller, paying no regard to rank and station. One woman, Martha the daughter of a wealthy prominent citizen and whose wedding dowry had been one million gold denarii, was seen picking grains of corn from the dung in the streets. Another account reveals the horror of the Roman siege of Jerusalem in A. D. 70. Hunger-crazed men broke into a house upon smelling roast meat, and were confronted by Maria, who was from the social élite of Jewish nobility. The men threatened to kill her if she refused to share her find, but when they went to seize the meat they found it was Maria's half-eaten baby. The daughters of Jerusalem heard Jesus say, 'For, behold, the days are coming, in the which they shall say, Blessed are the barren, and the wombs that never bare, and the paps which never gave suck. Then shall they begin to say to the mountains, Fall on us, and to the hills, Cover us' (Luke 23:29-30). That day had arrived.

The famine was not endured in silence. The hammering of the battering rams continued unabated day and night, providing a constant reminder, if one was needed, that Jerusalem's final obstacle would inevitably be breached, and the shrill whine of the projectiles overhead merely served to underline the fact. Thus in midsummer Titus' troops swarmed into the temple area and headed for the sacred territory where the remaining Jews, as crazed with fervour as they were with hunger, had gathered to fight the invaders to the bitter death they knew would be theirs.

The destruction of the temple

At this point Titus was confronted with a personal dilemma. His troops had virtually destroyed the rest of Jerusalem, but the temple had been built by Herod the Great in honour of the Cæsar and completed only four years earlier, after eighty-six years in construction. Destroying so magnificent an edifice might well be seen by his father in Rome as an insult. Titus, who himself would be made emperor nine years later, decided to ponder the matter. What he did not realize, nor could he possibly have understood, was God's plan for this symbol of Jewish corruption expressed in Jesus' words to an awe-struck band of disciples: 'See ye not all these things? Verily I say unto you, There shall not be left here one stone upon another, that shall not be thrown down' (Matt. 24:2).

Titus' mind was eventually made up for him. Although he had issued the order to spare the sanctuary one of his soldiers either had not heard it, or deliberately disobeyed it, and flung a lighted torch close to the most holy place. This swiftly turned into a raging fire, there being so much that was inflammable in the area. Although Titus made every effort through his men to eradicate the blaze it was of no avail. Those watching events from the hillsides saw a number of the Jewish renegades jumping into the flames as a final act of defiance against Rome, and perhaps also against Jehovah whom they had expected to come to their aid, even at so late an hour.

The aftermath

In the confusion which followed some of the leading Jews managed to get through the Roman lines with their followers and fled to Masada, the isolated mountain fortification overlooking the Dead Sea, where they joined others who had escaped earlier. Three years later, after a lengthy siege by the Tenth Legion, 960 of them committed mass suicide in what has since become one of the heroic epics of Jewish history.

By September of A. D. 70, Jerusalem's resistance was crushed. The following year, the captured survivors and proud heroes of a demoralized Israel were paraded in chains before the people of Rome as Titus received the public acclaim for his victory in Israel, albeit six months later than anticipated.

In the meantime, a thick pall of smoke overshadowed Jerusalem, and lingered as the legionaries walked through silent streets. The dead lay everywhere and even hardened warriors were sickened by the stench and the sight of thousands of bodies either piled high in corners, or lying where they had fallen weeks before. Tacitus, the Roman historian, suggests that there were over half a million people trapped by the siege, 97,000 of them taken away in chains, and that 115,800 rotting corpses were dragged through just one of Jerusalem's gates.

Prophecy fulfilled

Nobody could have disagreed with Jesus' words, spoken a generation before: 'These be the days of vengeance, that all things which are written may be fulfilled. But woe unto them that are with child, and to them that give suck, in those days! for there shall be great distress in the land, and wrath upon this people. And they shall fall by the edge of the sword, and shall be led away captive into all nations, and Jerusalem shall be trodden down of the Gentiles, until the times of the Gentiles be fulfilled' (Luke 21:22-24).

Some might ask at this point, what happened to the Christians throughout this national catastrophe? They were not in the city, but were living in safety at Pella (Kherbet-el-Fahil) seventy or so miles away in the north of the land near the Sea of Galilee — ironically, close to where Jesus grew up and lived during the early part of his ministry.

For forty years, the Christian communities within Israel had treasured the memories of their Lord and Saviour and the words of warning he had given, and they did not need to be old to have remembered them: 'Then let them which are in Judæa flee to the mountains; and let them which are in the midst of it depart out; and let not them that are in the countries enter thereinto' (Luke 21:21). God not only saves, he keeps! (1 Peter 1:5).